# HALLOWEEN
## —and—
# SATANISM

*PHIL PHILLIPS and*
*JOAN HAKE ROBIE*

# HALLOWEEN
## —and—
# SATANISM

## PHIL PHILLIPS and
## JOAN HAKE ROBIE

STARBURST PUBLISHERS

P.O. Box 4123, Lancaster, Pennsylvania 17604

**Phil Phillips,** evangelist/author, worked with Joan Hake Robie on three books— best-selling *Turmoil In The Toy Box, Halloween and Satanism,* and *Horror and Violence— The Deadly Duo In The Media.* Participating in over 200 interviews a year, Phil is a regular guest on Marlin Maddoux—*Point of View,* the 700 Club, and TBN. He has made guest appearances on Donahue, Sally Jesse Raphael, CNN, and has been interviewed by *Newsweek* and *USA Today.* His most recent books are *Dinosaurs, The Bible , Barney & Beyond, Angels, Angels, Angels—Embraced by the Light...Or...Embraced by The Darkness?* and *The Truth About Power Rangers.*

**Joan Hake Robie,** editor and ghostwriter of best-selling *Turmoil In The Toy Box (1) (Phil Phillips),* is author of fourteen books, which includes *Halloween And Satanism, Turmoil In The Toy Box II,* and *Horror And Violence—The Deadly Duo In The Media.* Joan has appeared on TV shows such as Geraldo Rivera, Sonja Live, People Are Talking, and Heritage Today. She has been a regular guest (as a conservative-moral activist) on The Morton Downey Jr. Show. Her radio shows include USA Radio, Christian Broadcasting Network and Moody Network's Open Line. Joan is a speaker and conducts seminars.

To schedule Author appearances write:
Author Appearances, Starburst Promotions, P.O. Box 4123,
Lancaster, Pennsylvania 17604 or call (717) 293-0939.

## Credits:

Cover art by Kerne Erickson.
Unless otherwise noted, all Scripture quotations are from the King James Version.

We, the Publisher and Authors, declare that to the best of our knowledge all material (quoted or not) contained herein is accurate; and we shall not be held liable for the same.

# HALLOWEEN AND SATANISM

First Printing, September 1987
Second Printing, January 1988
Third Printing, August 1988
Fourth Printing, August 1989
Fifth Printing, September 1990

Sixth Printing, July 1991
Seventh Printing, August 1992
Eighth Printing, August 1993
Ninth Printing, August 1994
Tenth Printing, August 1995

ISBN: 0-914984-11-X
Library of Congress Catalog Number 87-91287
Printed in the United States of America

This book is dedicated to all those who wish to be enlightened to the many devices of Satan, and to those who are already under his control — **You can be set free!**

# CONTENTS

# INTRODUCTION

If you question how the 'innocent' celebration of *Halloween* can be coupled with *Satanism,* or you think these writers are unnecessarily alarmed, YOU NEED TO READ THIS BOOK — it could save you or someone you love from the pitfalls of Satan. You need to know how *Horoscopes, the Ouija Board, Talismans, Tea-Leaf Reading, Tarot Cards, Good Luck Charms, Dungeons and Dragons* and many other so-called 'fun' things are really very 'deadly', and should be avoided. If you already are involved with any of these or other devices of Satan you need to know the truth. You need to learn how you can be set free. This book will enlighten you and lead you, step by step, into deliverance from any and all Satanic control.

Phil Phillips and Joan Hake Robie

# 1

# THE SPIRIT OF FEAR

The night outside was cold and damp; an eerie darkness hovered over the city. As I stumbled through the dimly-lit, closed-in room I bumped into the many others, who also were desperately struggling to find their way out of that dark and dismal place.

Suddenly, I felt a cold hand grab my arm.

"Let go of me!" I yelled as *fear* welled up within me.

I became wet with perspiration as I pulled away from the cold hand. Again it grabbed my arm. Again I pulled away. I leaped forward, only to look into the face of a horrible creature with 'blood' running out of its nose and mouth.

There was a lot of pushing and shoving in the room. I tried to leave.

"Ouch," I moaned, as the heel of a shoe crushed down on my foot.

"Get off my foot!" I yelled.

Pulling free, I managed to get out of that room, only to find myself in another equally dark and oppressive one. From a loft near the ceiling, the eyes of a black cat stared down at me. 'Owls', 'bats', and 'frogs' guarded that awful place.

Along with hundreds of other young people, I finally made my way out of that *haunted house*.

With the door swinging behind me I said to myself, "If this is *Halloween*, who needs it?"

Phil Phillips

*Fear is a debilitating force. It can cause one to lose the proper perspective of life. It can destroy the very life of a person. It can cause both physical and emotional illness. It can cause one to lose faith in God.*

Thirty-five year old Barbara reports, "One Sunday morning, as I stood among the throng of people gathered in the vestibule of the church, I began to panic. My heart began to pound loudly and the room seemed to swirl around me. I began to be overwhelmed with anxiety, and wanted to leave immediately, but my legs felt too weak to carry me. Feebly shaking the hands that were extended toward me, I made my way to the door and out to the steps. Fearing that I was having a heart attack, I stumbled to the parking lot and to my car. Once home, my husband insisted that I go to the doctor to determine what was wrong with me. As you might expect, the doctor assured me that nothing was wrong. I was embarrassed and yet I knew that my feelings were real."

The condition Barbara had is called *agoraphobia,* and is suffered by people everywhere. Agoraphobia literally means *a fear of open spaces or fear of the marketplace.* However, it is much more than this. It could best be defined as a 'fear of fear' or a 'fear of symptoms.' These fears lead to avoidance of those places or objects that invoke the fear. When this occurs one often limits normal activities. A restricted and avoidance behavior dominates this person's life.

In a recent study by the National Institute of Mental Health, phobias are a leading mental health problem in our country. But they are often believed to be another illness, as in Barbara's case. It is estimated that 20 million people suffer from phobias, with two million having phobias severe enough to drastically limit their normal every day lives. Agoraphobia is one of the most limiting of all phobias and may be affecting as many as one out of twenty people.

According to the Phobia Information Center of Dallas, Texas, sufferers describe the first attack as 'coming out of the blue' usually after a period of stress or illness, or after a loss or separation. These intense physical symptoms are followed by a 'panic' reaction, caused by increased adrenalin surging through the body. The physical reactions are similar to what one experiences if being chased by a bear. However, with agoraphobia there is no known reason to fear. The overwhelming symptoms occur suddenly and the symptoms themselves are perceived as a threat, causing panic to set in.

These feelings may occur only in those situations where they first appeared. For Barbara it was in a church crowd. Or they may spread into different areas. Conversely, these feelings of being trapped often escape the sufferer if he or she is with someone they trust, such as a spouse.

## Fear Is Not of God

In today's society, fear is the entertainment industry's 'stock in trade.' Most of us are all cognizant of the fact that fear plays a leading role in television and theater productions. People want to be, 'scared to death', and are usually not knowledgeable, or don't care, about the ill effects that fear, whether in reality or in 'fun', has on our health and general well-being. While we have had the *Dracula* of the past as well as the present, today the movie industry promotes fear-inducing films in vivid color and in the most explicit manner.

A dramatic change took place in 1981 when *horror began to be mixed with comedy.* An example is *American Were-wolf in London.* Other movies which fall into this category are: *Gremlins* and *Poltergeist.*

If fear is not of God, then why do Christians still attend these horror movies that were especially designed to generate and promote fear? Horror movies, from their very inception, have dealt and continue to deal with the occult and the demonic supernatural. In fact, they have successfully made heroes and gods of occult figures, even to the point of making these figures and their powers desirable.

The frequency with which occult powers and practices are portrayed in not only horror movies, but even in movies that are considered to be innocent entertainment, is increasing at a frenzied rate of speed. For example, *the most popular movie of 1982 was E.T. This movie, which generated over 313 million dollars in revenue, introduced to the world a fetus-looking creature who had the power to physically heal, levitate and create a psychic bond between himself and his little human friend, Elliot.*

THE GHOSTBUSTERS (toy and cartoon)

*The most popular movie of 1984 was Ghostbusters, which was acclaimed as the comedy of the year. In this movie a woman becomes demon-possessed. She and a man have sex on an altar to the goddess 'Zoul.' This act causes the goddess to manifest herself, and she appears out of a golden pyramid, then, with supernatural power that flows from her hands she transforms the couple into gargoyles.*

One of the most popular movies of 1986 was *Golden Child,* starring Eddie Murphy. Although this movie was touted as a comedy, it makes *E.T.* and *Ghostbusters* look like 'a Sunday afternoon walk through the park.' This popular movie graphically depicts a demon who goes to hell to communicate directly with Satan. Also depicted is a child who is the *Dalai Lama of Tibet,* which was presented as the equivalent of Christ. Dalai Lama of Tibet was believed to be here to save the world, which supposedly Christ had failed to do because He was killed by Satan.

Can you not see the perpetration of this great lie? Sad to say, many people cannot or will not defend their faith against the multi-million dollar productions presented by Hollywood.

## Fear Leads To The Occult

Dr. Grace H. Ketterman in her book, *You and Your Child's Problems: How to Understand and Solve Them* makes an excellent point concerning fear. A noted medical doctor, Ketterman says that a tragic by-product of fear in the lives of children as early as pre-adolescence is the interest and involvement in supernatural occult phenomena: Ellen had learned of witchcraft from a superstitious grandmother when she was only four-years-old. As soon as she learned to read, Ellen studied articles and books on occult beliefs and practices. Her 'inner' and 'outer' worlds became weird and extremely frightening to her.

By the time Dr. Ketterman ministered to then twelve-year-old Ellen, the child was convinced that love and caring are weak feelings. She was so entrenched in fear that she actually had been practicing a form of witchcraft.

Imagine, this little girl practicing witchcraft at the tender age of twelve? Unfortunately, there are thousands of others like Ellen. Let us stop Satan in his tracks by being *aware* and *putting on the armor of God!*

*Put on the whole armour of God, that ye may be able to stand against the wiles of the devil.* Ephesians 6:11

*For ye have not received the spirit of bondage again to fear; but ye have received the Spirit of adoption, whereby we cry, Abba, Father.* Romans 8:15

*There is no fear in love; but perfect love casteth out fear; because fear hath torment. He that feareth is not made perfect in love.* I John 4:18

If fear is not of God, then *Halloween* is not just a time for innocent fun.

# 2

# A CELEBRATION
# OF DEATH

*If you thought Halloween was a time for cornstalks, pumpkins, apples, and apple cider — a time for children dressed in cute costumes of witches, goblins, ghosts or devils to knock at your door calling, "TRICK OR TREAT", you had better 'wise up!' There is more to Halloween . . . much more!*

Did you know that Halloween is a day 'witches' celebrate above all other days? Witches have eight major festivals throughout the year. One at both *solstices* and *equinoxes*, and at four other times during the year: *February* — announcing Spring, *April* — welcoming Summer, *August* — heralding harvest (Fall), and *October* awaiting Winter. The major witchcraft festival is October 31 or *Halloween.*

*Witchcraft is not child's play. It is an abomination in the eyes of God.* From 1575 to the 1700's many people were burned at the stake for their real or suspected involvement in witchcraft. Yet, today witchcraft has gained acceptability by many people. Even the Internal Revenue Service has given tax exempt status to the church of Wicca (the official church of witchcraft), which means your gift to witchcraft is a tax deductible, charitable donation of a religious nature, the same as if you were tithing to the church of Jesus Christ. In the eyes of the U.S. Government there is no difference.

17

## The Halloween Witch

The Halloween Witch is a strange-looking female in black cloak and peaked hat riding a broomstick along with her symbolic cat. Her name is derived from the Saxon word *wica,* which means 'wise one.'

HALLOWEEN Witch

Artists of the Middle Ages often showed witches preparing to fly off to one of their Sabbaths. It was believed that angels and devils were supposed to be able to fly, so it was easy to believe that witches, too, could fly. The broomstick, originally made from a stalk of the broom plant with a bunch of leaves at the head, was said to be used by poor witches who went on foot. The broom or pole was used to vault over brooks, streams or thorny patches. Due to its use as an indoor cleaning supply, the broom became the symbol of women. Before setting out for a Sabbath, witches would rub 'sacred' ointment called *Ungent* into their pores. One ingredient in the ointment confused the mind. Another speeded up the witch's pulse. Still another numbed the feet. This gave them a feeling of flying. If they had been fasting, the ointment seemed to make them feel even giddier. Bat blood was another ingredient in that ointment. In England, during initiation ceremonies, new witches were sometimes blindfolded, smeared with the Ungent, then placed on a broom.

The peeling of church bells was believed to be a defense against aerial witches. In Slav countries people used to fire muskets at the clouds, screaming as they did so, "Curse, curse Herodius, thy mother is a heathen damned of God", while others laid scythes and billhooks on the ground, edge upwards, to assure that the witches would not have a safe landing.

The black of a witch's cloak reminds us that Halloween is a 'festival of the dead.'

## The Seventh Century

*All Saints' Day* (All Souls' Day), a day the seventh century church set aside in memory of early Christians who died for their beliefs, was first celebrated in the month of May. (By the year 900 the date had been changed to November 1.)

Another name for All Saints' Day was *All Hallows.* October 31 was known as *All Hallows' Eve,* which was later shortened to *Halloween.*

The Archbishop of Canterbury, England, set punishments for "those who goeth about in the masque of a stag of bull-calf . . . those who by their craft raise storms . . . sacrifice to demons . . . consulteth soothsayers who divine by birds."

The people described by the Archbishop worshipped a *horned god.* This god usually was a goat, bull or ram, but sometimes a man or woman wearing skins and the head of an animal.

During their magical rites they would dance about in a

circle, barking and howling. At midnight, using a bronze sickle, they would gather herbs. Spells were cast or enemies bewitched by sticking thorns into a wax model of the person. They also brewed love potions and concocted poisons.

Horned God

The skins of snakes and the saliva and intestines of animals were dropped into their cauldrons. The wings and entrails of bats also went into their brews. At the end of the ceremony they sacrificed and ate the animal god. Their rites and ceremonies expressed their closeness to all animal life, and their desire to help it grow.

Although Christianity was spreading, the religion of the horned god continued in its popularity. To some, the services of the Catholic church, with their rigid formalism, held less excitement for the people than the witch cult. Even after the people of Brittany became Christians, worship of the dead continued. During the Middle Ages, stone lighthouses, called

'Lanterns of the Dead', gave protection against malicious ghosts on All Hallows' Eve.

### The Tenth Century

Many of the followers of witchcraft were women, due in part to the fact that society looked upon women as being the property of their husbands but in the witch cult they were looked upon as equals. In the *tenth century*, King Edgar of England admitted that witchcraft was more popular than Christianity. It was then that it's followers became known as *witches*.

While All Hallows' Eve originally had been a strictly Christian holiday, the pagan influences from earlier traditions gradually crept in while the Catholic church's influence waned. Soon Halloween became a secular observance, and many customs and practices developed.

### The Fourteenth Century

The *fourteenth century* saw the rise of suspicion and occult practices. In 1307, Philip IV of France is reported to have accused the Order of Knights Templar of heresy and homosexual vice. True or not, the greed of Philip IV for the Order's wealth and the fact that the knights' confessions were extorted by torture and threats have made many historians suspicious. One of the accusations leveled against the Templars was that they worshipped an idol named Baphomet.

Baphomet was sometimes said to be a head stuffed with a human head, sometimes a head with three faces, sometimes a human skull. The knights reportedly believed that the head was the source of their riches and also the source of fertility: it was believed to make the trees blossom and the earth produce crops. There were supposed to be several of these heads, kept at different Templar centers. One was described as being made of metal and having a face like a human face with curly black hair.

## Pan

Pan, the goat-footed deity of the Arcadians (famous hunters), was said to wander through woodland to glades accompanied by dancing nymphs; a shepherd god, he was also said to have the ability to cause sudden terror among both herds and men.

## Esbats

*Esbats* were weekly meetings held by the witches of a village. During this time the witches would gather in a home or in the open for instruction in magic. Magical rites and ceremonies were performed by the *coven,* a band of men and women from a district under the rule of a grand master. In England, covens were made up of thirteen people, twelve witches and the master.

## Sabbaths

Several times a year, witches would gather for their Sabbath. The Blocula in Sweden was one such place. Another was the Puy-de-Dome in France. The Hartz mountain region of Germany was the most famous sacred spot for witches. *It wasn't until the eighteenth century that maps of Germany stopped showing witches hovering over this spot.*

## May Day

*May Day,* a day celebrating the inauguration of the second half of the Celtic year and a symbol of rebirth and greenery, whose rites were believed to convey the power to endow crops and women with fertility and good luck, was one of the most important witches' Sabbaths. The central figure of the celebration was the maypole or May tree; in England this was the white hawthorn, which possessed supernatural powers and symbolized the transition from Spring to Summer. In America it was the evergreen arbutus.

The ceremony, which continued until the early 19th century, was described as a ritual contest between the Queen of Winter (a man dressed in woman's clothes) and a female Queen of the May. The same basic idea was also represented in the better-known ritual marriage between the May bridegroom and the May bride, which has been supposed to symbolize the union of Spring and vegetation.

The witches in attendance vowed to obey their god, the 'master' disguised as an animal. They kissed him on whatever

Horned God with Witches

part of his body he chose, and paid homage by turning

*widdershins* — from west to east — a certain number of times. They then consecrated their children to the god and thanked him as the source of food and life itself.

Witch couples were married at initiation ceremonies for new witches. After the religious ceremonies, they took part in feasting, chanting and dancing 'jumping' dances. They believed that the higher the witches jumped the higher the crops would grow.

Puritans opposed celebrations like May Day, calling them pagan worship. Suppressed during this Puritan time, these celebrations re-emerged at the Restoration. May Day rites continued through the 18th century and into the 19th.

## Magic

Early magicians in their search for knowledge tried to understand the forces of nature and then control them. The sorcerers believed that by painting a picture of something happening they could make it happen. This was called *imitative magic.*

In order to cast a 'spell' on an enemy, the sorcerer would steal a piece of that person's clothing, a lock of hair, or a piece of fingernail. If the enemy found out, he would become deathly sick with fear and maybe even die from that fear. This was called *contagious magic.*

Burning or sticking pins into a miniature model of the enemy would bewitch or kill the person. This was known as *sympathetic magic.*

Those who participated in witchcraft (sorcerers) were experts at mixing medicines as well as poisons. Their unusual knowledge of plant and animal products seemed almost 'magical.' Sorcerers were called upon to end dry spells, cloudiness, or too much rain.

## The Celts

The Celts worshipped the sun and used it in their worship. The name of the sun god was **Muck Olla.**

Sun Worship

The worship of the sun led from the Mediterranean westward and northward into Spain, France, the west of Britain and Ireland, north Germany, Denmark and southern Sweden. Its evidence consists of a trail of vast stone structures, *megaliths;* which can be seen at Stonehedge and Carnac in Brittany. Most megalith-builders were also sun worshippers.

## Druids

The earliest celebrations of Halloween began among the Celts, who lived more than 2,000 years ago in what is now England, Ireland, Scotland, Wales and northern France. The ancient Druids, in Britain, France, Germany and the Celtic countries celebrated the *Vigil of Samhain* in honor of their god, *Samhain,* lord of the dead. Halloween acquired sinister significance with ghosts, witches, hobgoblins, black cats, fairies, and demons of all kinds said to be roaming about the land. Research of the scope and nature of the Celtic traditional lore believed to be possessed by the Druids leads us to believe that the Druids were divided into two groups: one relating to *metaphysical* speculation and beliefs about the *supernatural,* and the other dealing with practical knowledge, including that involved in the organization of a calendar.

These pagan Celts believed that evil spirits lurked about as the sun god grew pale and Samhain grew stronger. By lighting great bonfires on the hillsides, on the Vigil of Samhain, they hoped to scare away the evil spirits of those who had died the previous year. It was believed that on this day the souls of the dead would rise from the grave to haunt those who were living. In order to please Samhain, the Druids held cruel fire rites. Prisoners of war, criminals, or animals were burned alive in odd-shaped baskets. By observing the way they died, the Druids saw omens of the future, good and bad. In addition, on this important day all the cooking fires were extinguished in the kitchens around the land. New fires were then lit from the great bonfire to honor the coming new year. By waving burning wisps of plaited straw aloft on pitchforks, people tried to frighten off demons and witches. Just in case waving of burning wisps didn't work, the Druids also put on grotesque and terrifying costumes. They believed that if you dressed in a horrible

Fire Worship

enough fashion and went trooping around with the spirits all night, they would think you were one of them and do you no harm.

The Celts believed that when these spirits came to your house, if you did not *treat* them, they would *trick* you.

Many of the Halloween legends and customs of today have come from the Celts. Even to this day, many of those who live in the countryside of Scotland and Ireland, where the Druid religion lasted longer than anywhere else in the Celtic region, build huge bonfires. When the last fires die out, the people race each other down the hills shouting,

Modern-Day Druids

"The Devil gets the last one down!"

Halloween was also a time for divinations, especially concerning marriage, luck, health, and death. In Scotland young people assembled for games and to pull shoots out of the ground to ascertain which of them would marry during the year and in what order the marriages would occur. It was on this day that the Devil's help was sought for such purposes.

In the first century before Christ, Roman armies invaded Britain and Gaul (as France was known at that time), and made them part of the Roman Empire. Many Roman soldiers stayed on in the new territories.

The Romans had a festival for the dead in late October, the *Fernalia*. In November they honored *Pomona*, goddess of orchards. The two festivals gradually blended with the Druid Samhain.

28

### Stonehenge

The Druids were thought to be the builders of England's 'Stonehenge' to be used as a sun worshipping temple and site for human sacrifice. The stone carving was used to determine the best day to appease their god. The date decided upon was October 31. (Many 18th and 19th century authors produced lengthy statements of proof of the Druid involvement, and many 20th century authors accept this explanation.)

However, archeology contends that Stonehenge was not built by the Druids, as some believed, but existed at a far earlier period. There is a difference of opinion as to the purpose of Stonehenge, whether it served as a temple, observatory or political center.

Stonehenge

Stonehenge consists of a number of giant standing stones, some in pairs with lintel stones across their tops, and also many fallen stones — all placed with sufficient symmetry to indicate that what we now see may not have been the whole of the construction in its original state. Stonehenge is an eerie place rising out of the empty Salisbury plain.

Legend has it that Stonehenge is a monument erected in memory of a number of ancient British nobles, murdered by the treachery of Hengist, the Saxon, during a supposed truce. Magician 'Merlin' advised the king of the Britons to use vast stones brought from a structure he called 'Giant's Dance', in Ireland. These stones were thought to possess magical force but it took the powers of Merlin, after the routing of the Irish, to convey these powers to England.

## Glastonbury

Built on the site of the ancient Isle of Avalon, Glastonbury is reputed to be not only the first Christian foundation in Britian but the last resting place of King Arthur. Glastonbury in Somerset, famed for its ruined Abbey, is dominated by the Tor, a hill rising about 500 feet above sea level and commanding a wide expanse of low-lying country.

At the start of the Christian era, Glastonbury was merely an island encircled by rivers and lagoons. To the British Celts it was a place of great religious awe, the enchanted Isle of Avalon. Another name for it was the Isle of Glass.

Legend has it that in the First Century AD Joseph of Arimathea, the rich man who buried Christ, brought the Holy Grail to Avalon. Led by a 'vision', Joseph of Arimathea and his companies are said to have built the 'Old Church', dedicated to the Virgin and deeply respected. During the early Middle Ages, this church was still standing.

Glastonbury is the one place in Britain where Christianity has endured from the Apostolic age. It is a natural shrine, with a spiritual character which has always set Britain apart from the rest of Christendom.

## Snap Apple Night

Apples have long been a token of love and fertility. Early Hebrew women who wanted children washed themselves in water mixed with the sap of an apple tree. 'Eternal youth' was said to come to the Norse gods by the eating of apples.

At the first Halloween parties, people roasted and ate apples and bobbed for apples in tubs of water. If a boy came up with a dripping apple between his teeth, he was assured of the love of his girl.

*Snap Apple* was a game boys enjoyed. Each boy in turn sprang up and tried to bite an apple that was twirled on the end of a stick. The first to succeed would be the first to marry.

Peeling an apple and keeping the peeling in one long piece was supposed to tell a young girl about her future. The peeling is swung three times around the head, then thrown over the left shoulder. If the peeling falls unbroken, it is supposed to form the initial of the girl's future husband.

Apple seeds were also used to tell fortunes. Seeds named for two different sweethearts were stuck to a girl's eyelids. The length of time the seeds stayed on the eyelids showed which sweetheart was truer. Perhaps many a young girl twitched her cheek or winked one eye to help fate agree with her preferred choice.

When the English people first settled in America, some of them still continued the old custom of apple-ducking, apple-snapping, and girls tossing apple parings over their shoulders.

It was in *England* that Halloween was nicknamed *Nutcracker Night* or *Snap Apple Night*. Families would sit before great fires in the hearth, roasting nuts and eating apples. Then they would tell stories and play holiday games. During All Souls' Day celebrations, the poor people in England would walk from door to door begging for food. The term used for this was 'going a-souling.' In exchange for

31

special sweets, the poor would promise to say prayers for those of the family who had died.

Each year, more and more adults and children went around on All Souls' Day, seeking sweet buns, apples and money. As they walked through the streets of England they would chant:

> Soul, soul! for a soul cake!
> I pray, good mistress, for a soul cake!
> An apple or a pear, or a plum or a cherry.
> Any good thing to make us merry.
> One for Peter, two for Paul,
> Three for Him Who made us all.
> Up with the kettle and down with the pan.
> Give us good alms and we'll be gone.

A *soul cake* was a square bun decorated with currants. During this special holiday, bakers would fill their shops with soul cakes.

## Pulling the Kale

Unengaged girls in Scotland would go blindfolded to the vegetable garden and each pull up a stalk of kale. Then, they would return to the house and remove the blindfolds.

If the white stalk was closed it meant an elderly husband. An open green one meant a younger mate. The girl would taste the stem to determine if her husband's disposition would be bitter or sweet. In order to find out his name she would hang the stalk with a row of others above the door. If Mary's stalk hung third in line, and the third man to pass through the door was named John, Mary believed that her future husband would be named John.

A Halloween custom in *Ireland* was that cabbage stalks would be named for different people at the Halloween party. The cabbages were then examined. If a cabbage was clean and light it meant that the person would go to heaven. If the cabbage was darkened by frost it meant that the person would go to hell.

Halloween was a country holiday; but as more and more settlers moved to the cities, the custom of cabbage-pulling was forgotten.

## Halloween Foods

The great celebration of Halloween in Ireland was never complete without *caulcannon*, a dish made of mashed potatoes, parsnips, and onions, and with tiny objects inside another way of telling fortunes. If a person found a coin in his or her portion of the caulcannon it meant that they would find wealth. A thimble meant spinsterhood, a doll predicted children and a ring indicated marriage.

Scotch and Irish settlers held parties with a double meaning of Halloween 'a festival of the natural and the supernatural.' Their table would be set with a pumpkin filled with nuts, raisins, apples and other harvest fruits. There might be a pumpkin coach drawn by stuffed field mice. Inside the coach would be a tiny witch — *a symbol of magic.*

Next, while funeral music was playing, they would march to the table to a feast of gingerbread, doughnuts, pumpkin pie, cider, apples, nuts and buttered popcorn.

## The Jack-O-Lantern

A common symbol of Halloween is the Jack-O-Lantern (the name possibly was derived from that for a night watchman). Some people called them 'Lantern Men', Hob-O-Langer', 'Jack-O-Lantern', 'Will-O'-The-Wisp', or 'Will.' The 'Lantern Men' got their name from pale eerie lights that appeared over bogs and marshes in England. These ghostly lights, which bobbed along like a lantern in someone's hand, were called *Corpse Candles.* Fishermen in Kent would report that they saw Corpse Candles above a treacherous swampland on the coast.

Candles were said to be signals from the souls of men lost at sea. The signals were sent by the souls of men who wanted to be buried when their bodies were washed ashore. It was thought that if a bone or two could be found, the ghost would be laid to rest and the Corpse Candle put out. People were warned never to follow these strange lights because they would lead a person to a watery death in the deepest and most dangerous part of the swamp.

A more 'scientific' viewpoint of the Will-O'-The-Wisp is that called *ignis fatuus,* meaning *foolish fire.* There are two opinions of what this strange flickering of light may be: the flashing light of phosphorus like that of the firefly, or the spontaneous combustion from methane or marsh gas that burns so easily. This gas is given off by rotting plant and animal forms in places where there is little oxygen.

In Kent, England the story goes that one farmer told of being followed home by a Jack-O-Lantern. Shivering and shaking, the farmer said he jumped into bed and pulled the covers over his head. When he finally got the courage to get up and look out the window he saw the Jack-O-Lantern at his window.

The custom was that if you met a Jack-O-Lantern you had to immediately put out your own lantern lest Jack would dash it to pieces. If he came close enough to do that you had to throw yourself on the ground and hold your breath.

Some people imagined that Jack-O-Lanterns were the souls of sinners condemned to walk the earth till the end of time.

### A Man Named Jack

The story which accompanies the Jack-O-Lantern is that of a stingy Irish drunkard named 'Stingy Jack' who, one

Halloween, invited the Devil to have a drink.

"If you pay for it," the Devil replied.

"But you can change into any shape you choose," Jack protested. "Change yourself into a sixpence. After I've paid for the drink, you can change yourself back."

The Devil agreed. He mumbled a spell, disappeared, and there on the counter was a shiny new sixpence.

But Stingy Jack quickly placed the coin into his pocket, where a silver cross prevented the Devil from getting out. "If you'll let me alone for a year, I'll let you out," Jack promised.

The Devil agreed and was released.

Jack intended to reform; to take his pay home to his wife, and to go to church and give to the poor. But as soon as he was out of danger he went back to his old ways.

The next Halloween Jack met the Devil on a lonely road. "He's come for my soul!" thought Jack. This time he tricked the Devil into sparing his soul for ten years. But before a year had passed, Jack died. Turned back at the gates of heaven, Jack made his way to the gates of hell.

"Go away," shouted the Devil.

"Where can I go?" asked Jack of the Devil.

"Go back to where you've come." ordered the Devil. "You tricked me, and made me promise not to claim your soul."

Jack began his trek back through wind and darkness. As Jack trudged on, eating a turnip as he went, the Devil threw him a live coal out of the fires of hell. In desperation to find his way, Jack put the live coal inside the turnip. Ever since that time Jack is said to be roaming the face of the earth with his *Jack-O-Lantern*, searching for a place of rest.

*The story of Jack is said to be the origin of the 'globe-faced pumpkins' that sit on the porches, fenceposts and in the windows of American homes at Halloween. The American Jack-O-Lantern is a hollowed-out pumpkin carved in the appearance of a grinning demonic face with a lighted candle inside. In Ireland celebrators carved out the centers of large rutabagas, turnips, and potatoes.*

For Scotland it was a turnip which they called 'bogies' and carried to scare away witches. In parts of England children carry 'punkies', which are large beets known as *mangel-wurzels*. These are hollowed out and have a window through which the candle shines.

## Customs

Until the present century, masked figures, led by Lair Bhan (which means white mare), a leader wearing a white robe and a horse-head mask, (the horse was sacred, a symbol of fertility, to Muck Olla), went begging from farm to farm, blowing cows' horns to let the villagers know they were coming.

Gathering more followers as he went, Lair Bhan would call out the head of the household. Then he recited a long string of verses that told the farmer that his good fortunes were due to the goodness of Muck Olla. The verses recited described the damage Muck Olla would do to a farmer's house or barn if the farmer refused to give something. If the farmer wanted to prosper during the coming year, he had better make a generous contribution to the spirit. At the end of the evening, the masqueraders went home, loaded down with eggs, butter, corn, cheese, and potatoes. Of course most farmers opened their purse strings so as not to suffer famine, drought or illness. Some farmers even gave gold coins.

Not all 'dressing up' on Halloween comes from pagan rituals. It also has its origins in the Roman Catholic Church, the main church of Ireland. On All Hallows, many churches staged plays called *pageants* for the benefit of their members. Each pageant participant dressed up as the *patron saint* of his special guardian. Those who did not play the part of a 'holy one' played the parts of devils.

The procession then marched from the church out into the churchyard, where the play might continue until late in the evening. Soon, nearly all of Ireland thought of October 31 as a night for dressing up in costume. For some, it was a means to satisfy Muck Olla, for others, a way to celebrate All Hallows.

Gradually, Halloween costumes changed from the traditional horses, saints, and devils to witches, ghosts and goblins. To some, the costumes were believed to scare away the real demons.

In time, the custom of dressing up in costume and the custom of going from house to house in search of 'treats' combined.

Belgian children once stood beside little shrines in front of their homes, begging for money to buy cakes. They were taught that for each cake they ate, the suffering of one dead soul would be eased.

*Just as people once offered gifts of food to the spirits, people today offer treats to the children who represent them. In reality, the lighted Jack-O-Lanterns the children carry are really a symbol of the fires and torches of former Halloweens and of the ancient Samhain.*

So is the beginning of TRICK OR TREAT!

# 3

# THE STRANGE AND THE SUPERNATURAL

'Creatures of the night' 'deception', the strange, and supernatural, characterize Halloween, the celebration of death.

### The Owl

Screech owls nest in hollow trees and seldom give any sign of their presence — that is, until nighttime. Suddenly, without warning, the weird sounding creature begins his hollow whistle. Since the sound is 'witchlike', it brought fear to those who passed by. To the superstitious, the sound of the screech owl meant impending disaster or death.

While in Greece the owl was considered deity, to the ancient Romans it was considered evil. Europeans of the Middle Ages feared the glassy star and eerie call of the owl. To the Greek goddess of wisdom, Athene, the owl was a *familiar*. A familiar is a spirit often in animal form, believed to act as a servant, as to a witch.

### The Toad

One who lives on a farm knows that the 'toad' is an ever-present inhabitant of gardens, under porches, in fields and along the roadside. This creature, in wet weather or at dawn or dusk, can be found creeping out to stalk cutworms, snails, and moths.

Toads were considered poisonous and people noticed

that when a dog chased a toad the dog might come away with sore eyes or a sore mouth. When people handled a toad they noticed that their own eyes or nose would itch or burn. Today we know that a toad does not spit out poison, but to protect itself when in danger, it gives off a certain substance which can irritate the eyes, nose or mouth. A toad absorbs water through its skin, thus it can change from small to large, or from large to small.

A toad can be tamed and fed on bread and water. It can live for as long as thirty-five years.

> Round about the caldron go;
> In the poisoned entrails throw.
> Toad, that under the cold stone,
> Days and nights hast thirty-one
> Swelter'd venom sleeping got,
> Boil thou first i' the charmed pot!

Witches told of mixing the spittle of a toad or bits of its body into their brews. The poem above is about a toad boiled in the bubbling cauldron of the three Weird Sisters in William Shakespeare's play, *Macbeth*.

### Cats

During the thousands of years that the cat has lived among human beings it has been given the place of *deity* or *cursed as a demon*. The cat was considered 'sacred' in ancient Egypt; and *Bast*, the cat-headed goddess was believed to be the ruler of the city of Bubastis which is situated to the east of the Nile Delta. Cats were first tamed here to keep the grain storehouses free of mice and rats. Furniture and jewelry were designed in the shape of cats as well as statues carved like cats. To kill a cat was to risk death. The Greek historian, Diodorus Siculus, described how a Roman, who had committed this crime, was murdered by a mob despite the pleadings of high Egyptian officials. If a cat died its owner went into mourning, shaving his eyebrows and performing elaborate funeral rites. On the banks of the Nile cat cemeteries were established where the 'sacred' animals were mummified and buried together with vast quantities of cat mascots and bronze cat effigies.

Witches with Cats

The Roman goddess, Diana, sometimes took on the shape of a cat, and the chariot of Freya, the Scandinavian fertility goddess, was drawn by cats. This reverence of the cat was due, not so much to the animal's importance as the guardian of the granaries against mice, or to its role as the traditional enemy of the serpent, but to the beauty of the cat's eyes, which seemed to be reminiscent of the moon.

'Hecate' was a goddess of the ancient Greeks and Romans. Her purpose was to rule over witches, wizards, and ghosts. Hecates's priestess was a woman who turned into a cat.

Cats were carried aboard ships on the Mediterranean Sea by the Phoenicians. In Western Europe, cats were traded for precious tin. To Freya, the Norse goddess of beauty, love, and marriage, and of the dead, the cat was sacred. She was said to have been entitled to one-half of the warriors slain in battle, and would come for the dead in a chariot drawn by cats.

An Italian legend tells of a cat that gave birth to kittens beneath the manger of the Christ child. But the cat was not destined to be venerated in Christian Europe, for the Church with its hatred of paganism reduced the status of the cat to that of a devil.

To the Druids, cats were dreaded as human beings changed into animals by evil powers. That is the reason they were woven into baskets that were thrown into the Samhain fires.

Says Patricia Dale-Green, author of *Cult of the Cat*, "Like the moon it (the cat) comes to life at night, escaping from humanity and wandering over the housetops with its eyes beaming out through the darkness." "Many people believed the cat was the child of the moon and it was said that 'the moon brought forth the cat'."[1]

The changeableness of the pupils of the eye, which in the daytime is a mere narrow line, dilatable at night to a luminous globe, is the link from which this idea is thought to have originated. The 'magic' of the eyes of the cat led some to

Cat with Upside Down Crucifix

believe that cats were seers with strong mediumistic powers. In the East some believe that the cat bears away the souls of the dead; and in West Africa, it is believed that at death the human soul passes into the body of a cat.

## The Halloween Cat
In a classroom where children are asked to draw Halloween pictures of their own choosing, almost everyone draws the most popular symbols of the holiday, namely, a witch, a Jack-O-Lantern, or a black cat. Yet few parents realize the

true meaning of the celebration of Halloween or that there really are 'witches.' People used to go around accusing one another of being a witch. They believed that witches could change into cats themselves. Since everything looks dim and shadowy after dark, all cats looked black. Even though a cat serving as a witch's 'familiar' could be any color, as time went on, a witch's cat was thought of as being black. When a cat was found guilty of being a witch's 'familiar' it was killed along with the witch. Black cats were believed by some to be symbols of the evil (familiar) spirits that embody animals. The black cat was said to become a 'horse' to take the people to the great Halloween party. Each person who is involved in this 'worship' on Halloween is said to have a 'familiar spirit.' Thus, an innocent cat was suspected of being a witch in disguise, especially on Halloween.

Some of the sayings of these superstititous people were:

"A cat that sits with its back to the fire is raising a storm."

"Never let a cat into the same room with a corpse. It might be a demon and turn the dead soul into a vampire."

Among five witches accused of tormenting a certain English family was Elizabeth Dickson, whose 'familiar' was a white cat. An eight-year-old child by the name of Tomas Rabbet reported that his mother kept several "spirites", one of them "like a little grey cat."

## The Bat

The bat is an animal with leather-like wings and hideous appearance. One species, the *vampire bat,* is a notorious drinker of blood. The bat has a unique ability to hunt its prey in total darkness. This is largely the reason the bat has had a frightening reputation as a creature of occult power.

The bat has taken on some of the significance of both the bird (symbol of the soul) and the demon (dweller in darkness). In medieval times it was thought that the Devil often

Vampire Show Advertisement

assumed the shape of a bat.

The bat became not only the totem animal of the men of an aboriginal tribe in New South Wales but also their sex symbol. It has been said that Central European girls enticed their reluctant lovers into their arms by the addition of a few drops of bat blood to the boy's beer. On occasion, bats have been honored with the status of gods.

The bat is a significant symbol of Halloween. There are 'bats' at almost every Halloween Party.

Vampire Kissing Woman

## Masks

A very popular Halloween custom is the wearing of masks, (false faces) . . . witch masks, devil masks, cat masks, bat masks, and the list goes on. People hide behind all sorts of 'masks.' Some hide behind 'hats' and still others, including many of today's youth, and others, hide behind dark sunglasses.

From earliest times, people all over the world have worn masks for all sorts of reasons . . . droughts, epidemics, or other disasters. They hoped that the demons who had brought the disaster would see the mask and think they were demons, too, and be frightened off. In many primitive societies a mask was more than a means of changing one's appearance; it was a link with the world of the spirits, a channel by which men could tap the forces of the supernatural. The wearing of a mask was believed to change a man's

46

Mask, Bat, Owls, Snakes, Crystal Ball, etc.

identity and faculties, for the assumed appearance was believed to affect the wearer's inner nature and to assimilate it to that of the being represented by the mask.

During the Middle Ages, witches often put on masks or smeared their faces with soot and paint. People of nobility attending a witches' Sabbath would always arrive 'masked.'

Masks can be divided into two categories, the *religious* and the *profane*. Masks are worn by the dancers in the religious ceremonies of West African tribes. The theatre of ancient Greece is an example of the secular use of the mask. The use of the masks enabled actors to double and triple the number of parts they could play during any one performance.

Protection against supernatural dangers is a function of masks worn in certain ritual situations, such as at funerals. This is done 'in order to avoid recognition by the souls of the dead.' Masks are sometimes worn by 'warriors' to symbolize a superior power by identifying themselves with this force. While there are civilizations where the mask plays an important role in ritual activities, there are regions of the world where the wearing of masks is unknown.

Masks are worn in some initiation ceremonies of certain organizations. The wearer of the mask partakes of the power of the divinity or spirit which the mask symbolizes. Thus the wearer of the mask is believed to be elevated above the common mass of the uninitiated.

I ask you, **"Do Christians wear 'masks?' What kind of 'masks' do they wear?"**

## Goblins and Fairies

*Goblins and fairies, ugly, menacing little creatures who were believed to live underground or in dark places, had their origin in the pre-Celtic past. Like leprechauns, brownies and pixies, they stand for the evil spirits that were once thought to be present at the Vigil of Samhain and later on the eve of Halloween.* Goblins, also known as 'fairies', are believed to have started out as the ghosts of kings and heroes, with perhaps a touch of divinity in them. However, when the church bells rang and 'holy water' was sprinkled on them they were reduced to their present size.

In *Scotland,* a person would sit on a three-legged stool at the meeting of three roads. It was believed that this was where the fairies gathered and whispered the names of those who were to die during the year. By sitting at the meeting of three roads and waiting for the fairies, people could learn the names of the ill-fated ones. People believed that if they would throw a piece of clothing to the fairies as they pronounced a name, it would take away the sentence of death.

To the *French,* these fairies were known as goblins. As All Saints Day drew near, French children would be warned,

**"The goblins will get you if you don't watch out!"**

Fairies were not exactly the figment of the imagination. They were a dark-skinned people who lived in northern Europe and the British Isles. They were conquered by the Celtics in Britain and by the Germanic tribes in northern Europe.

In Britain, little people, who were about four and one-half feet in height and wore green clothing that blended with the fields and forests, lived in hiding in forests or near forts and towns. The green clothing they wore helped protect them from those conquerors who continually stalked them. The chief defense of the little people was to shoot little stone arrows known as 'elf bolts.' Because of their cunning and swift ways and their size, the Celts thought these small people were fairies, who were believed to be evil.

Food put out at one's door at night was said to keep fairies from harming home and family. If any food was left in the morning it was thrown away lest it be poisoned. Some people believed that fairies were afraid of iron, thus iron became a protective charm against the fairies. An iron horseshoe was especially lucky because of its cresent shape, resembling the moon.

Through the centuries, fairies were believed to have been transformed into elves and goblins. On Halloween, church bells rang loudly to keep fairies away. If milk spilled or cream soured, fairies were blamed.

Storybook fairies with their dainty little wings look nothing like the fairies once known as 'goblins.' The fairies of English tradition were thought to have their own realm with king and queen and royal courts.

Belief in fairies has been explored by many people, and frequently explained, nevertheless, it is a subject that is most bewildering. One reason for the mystery surrounding these little people is the wide-spread belief that it is unlucky to speak of fairies.

The original word, fairy was 'fay', and is believed derived from the Latin word, 'fata', the individual fates of men, who were personified as supernatural women visiting the cradles of newborn children. The word, 'fay' meant enchanted or bewitched, and 'fay-erie' was used for both a state of enchantment and for an enchanted realm. The state became confused with the person, and 'fays' became 'fairies.' Since believers in fairies did not think it wise to use the name, 'fairy', other complimentary words were used supposedly to bring favor with the 'fairies.'

## Ghosts

Perhaps when you were a child you went out into your neighborhood dressed as a 'ghost.' After dark on Halloween figures draped in white sheets would be flitting from house to house. Halloween parties with the lights out, wails and moans coming from a closet, and thrilling stories made this 'let's pretend' activity a lot of fun.

But do you know what a 'ghost' really is?

Ghosts are thought by some to be *spirit apparitions* through which the souls of dead persons are said to manifest themselves. To others, a ghost is a **demon** spirit which has been unleashed by Satan to live in a certain environment. To still others, 'ghosts' are explained away by attributing strange happenings to natural causes.

A Halloween custom of the Scotch and Irish girls was known as *the wetting of the sark sleeve*. This had once been a rite to the Norse goddess, Freya.

The girl would wash a fine piece of linen cloth in a running stream. An hour before midnight she would hang the cloth up to dry before a fire. At half-past eleven, she would turn the cloth. At twelve o'clock the spirit of her future husband was supposed to appear.

Ghost in Graveyard

– – – –

The story goes that in Indiana in 1965 there appeared apparitions of a woman and a child who had supposedly died in a fire. Crowds of people, some armed with shotguns, would be seen roaming around the woods and the town trying to spot the ghosts. In spite of the suggestion that the 'apparitions' were a hoax, crowds still came.

– – – –

The *Lancaster New Era*, Lancaster, PA, Thursday, June 4, 1987 reports the Associated Press as the source for the following story:

"—Hundreds of people jammed a suburban street to watch the side of a vacant house, where some people say they have seen an image of the Virgin Mary at night."

The story goes that the shape of a human form with a halo around it appeared as darkness came. Despite the fact that the figure disappeared when the family across the street opened their bow window, most of the crowd remained.

"Yes, it's reflecting," said one spectator, "But why would it reflect in that kind of form?"[2]

. . . the mystery remains.

## Poltergeists

The word *poltergeist* came from a German folklore term: *polter* (a noise or racket), *geist* (a spirit or sprite), indicating a nature spirit of like status to an elf or goblin or 'things that go bump in the night.' Eventually the term came to be used for a variety of happenings: furniture moving around the house, flinging of mud and stones, as well as noises, bangs, raps, scratchings and sounds imitating the human voice.

## Rattling Bones

Masks, costumes, decorations, skulls, skeletons, which mean the same thing as ghosts, and creatures of the night, all are reminders that Halloween is a celebration of the dead.

In past centuries, when the length of life was much shorter, it was the hope of a future and better life with which people consoled one another. A 'skull and crossbones' was not considered to be as eerie as it is today. In fact, many tombstones bore this sign.

To this day in Mexico, during the *Days of the Dead* celebration, holiday toys such as skeletons with moveable legs and toy coffins that release a skeleton Jack-In-The-Box are sold on the streets. Other jewelry items are likely to include tiepins in the shape of a skeleton with dangling ribs.

– – – –

In the past, every town or village had at least one old deserted house that was believed to be haunted . . . reports of persons hearing tapping on walls and the sound of footsteps, or wailing which they felt for sure was coming from more than the wind was not uncommon. Everyone avoided passing by a *haunted house*, especially at night, and on Halloween.

In some towns and villages people had what was known as *ghost animals*. The churchyard might be haunted by a hound as big as a calf or a white rabbit, with one huge eye. If you were unfortunate to pass by one of these creatures or if you heard it howling, it was a warning of death.

**The Hopi Indians summon the dead to a summer solstice festival, a time when the sun is highest in the heavens.**

**Relatives of the dead in Naples, Italy, pencil their names on the tombs and leave calling cards on All Souls Day.**

**Near Indonesia, on the island of Bali, ancestral spirits are believed to return during the first five weeks of the Buddhist year.**

**In Latin America, Halloween is not celebrated the same way it is celebrated in America. For centuries, Halloween was a night of ghosts. A time when men and boys went from house to house, singing albanzas to the spirits of the dead. These men and boys stayed together and avoided lonely roads.**

Families, where children had died, would set out candies, cakes and toys for their child angel. Some families would set off firecrackers to guide their *angelito* back home.

Except for a few isolated places, such customs and rites for the Days of the Dead are no longer celebrated in most of Latin America.

### Haunted Houses

The Lord does not give us the spirit of fear, He does not want us to seek after 'strange' and 'supernatural' happenings. Yet there are Christian youth groups all over the country who visit 'haunted houses.'

One pastor declares, *"Haunted houses are places where demons live. This whole idea of children dressing up like ghosts and vampires is actually a mask worn by Satan to make reality seem like the ridiculous."*

Are we, as believers in Jesus Christ, following His example when we portray werewolfs and devils? Or are we to portray the Jesus of the Bible? Should we, as spiritual leaders, create in young people a spirit of fear?

A psychic researcher who is said to be America's foremost magician, Milbourne Cristopher, believes that haunted houses have a 'natural' explanation: "There are sounds in old houses that are not made by human hands or human voices. They are heard during storms or at certain seasons of the year, or in some cases on specific days and at specific times. When the sounds persist, rumors spread that houses are haunted, and they are difficult to sell or rent."[3]

An undated clipping, preserved by Houdini, reports such a story. In Union, New York, seven miles from Binghamton, a once attractive two-story cottage was deteriorating. Paint peeled and cracked from its clapboards, grime clouded its remaining windows. Hinges, long unoiled, creaked, and the floors squeaked if a youngster, intrigued by the empty building, forced open a door and ran through the rooms. The neglected frame cottage was owned by J. W. McAdam of New York City. For two and a half years a man named Hakes had rented it. Neither he, his wife, nor his two children noticed anything peculiar during their occupancy.

Edgar Williams was the next tenant. He and his wife were the first to report that something unusual was taking place. It did not happen often, Williams told the real estate agent, but whenever a high wind swept across the property, bending the branches of trees, a wailing cry would echo through the upper floor. It was impossible to sleep then, he went on; his wife became so agitated that he thought her terror might affect her mind.

The agent went through the house, but could find nothing that might produce the weird sound. Shortly after this, the Williamses moved out. The next tenant had not been told of the strange noise. Less than a month later, he too was in to see the real estate man. He asked if anything odd had ever happened in the house. A murder, perhaps? The agent assured him that to the best of his knowledge nothing of this nature had ever taken place within the four walls. Then the tenant admitted that his wife too had heard the shrill shriek in the night; and she thought it came from the garret. The agent made another trip to the house. This time he thoroughly examined the garret on the pretext that the roof might need repair. Again, his search for a clue to the mystery was unsuccessful. In less than a week the house was vacant.

Three more families lived briefly in the cottage, all heard the strange, wailing cries. By now the story had spread through the area. It was impossible to rent the haunted house. Uncared for, it gradually took on an appearance that only a ghost would relish.

Early in December a man visited the real estate office and asked if the place which he had heard was haunted could be rented for a short period. The agent, delighted that interest was being expressed in a piece of property he had thought would never produce another penny, answered warily, "Yes, the house is available, but as to the haunting stories, they are sheer nonsense." The stranger put him straight. He was interested in a haunted house; he was investigating spiritualism and would like a week to study the sounds the people in that part of the state attributed to a ghost. The agency gave him access to the cottage for seven days without charge. When the man returned to the real estate office again, the rental agent was expecting the same old story of cries in the night. He asked: "Have you laid the ghost to rest?" His visitor replied: "I have, and here it is." The man reached in his pocket and took out a small metal object he had found in the garret. He displayed it on the palm of his hand. It was a toy — a child's whistle, with a hole on the side.

"This had been fastened in a knothole," he said, "and was directly opposite a broken pane of glass. When the wind blew hard, it caused a draft, and the wild shrieks your tenants heard were the natural result."[4]

Who would have guessed that one of the Hakes children, while playing in the garret, had plugged a hole with the whistle, or that a blast of wind would make it sound? Yet there are many accounts of how strange sounds in old houses have been made in the past. The whistle in Union, New York, was something new, but the currents of air have accounted for other mysterious noises throughout the years.

Despite the fact that there are explainable 'natural causes' for what is thought to be *ghost* activity, there are situations where this theory does not hold true. Take, for example, the following story told by author Allen Spraggett:

"Believe in ghosts? If not, how would you explain this true story?

One winter night, in northern Ontario, Canada, during the early days of World War II, a middle-aged widow awakened from a troubled sleep to see her younger brother standing at the foot of her bed.

The eerie thing was that the woman knew her brother was in England serving with the Royal Canadian Air Force.

Yet she saw him clearly, dressed in his pilot's flying suit, his face deathly pale and solemn beyond description. The effect was horrific. The woman screamed. Abruptly the strange phantasm vanished.

When the woman's three teen-aged children rushed into the room, they found her sobbing, "He's dead, I know he's dead."[5]

The premonition proved to be correct. Sometime later, word came that the brother's *Spitfire* had been shot down over the English Channel on the same day — possibly at the same hour — that the woman saw the spectral figure in her room.

This story was told to me by one of those intimately involved — the woman's son, who was a member of a church of which I was pastor." (Allen Spragett, *The Unexplained,* Signet Mystic Books, New York 1967.)

Another pastor reports this experience: "A few years ago, late in the month of October, I was ministering in a small Texas town. One afternoon I decided to do some sightseeing. As I drove down one road I looked to one side and saw something that astonished me. It was an old turn-of-the-century church building, but it was neither its wonderful architecture nor its beautiful stained glass windows that caught my eye and nearly took my breath away. Instead of the beauty, what astounded me was that in front of the building were giant wooden doors with beautiful glass windows above them, and in those windows were pictures of ghosts, witches, and even the Devil himself. A sign outside the church read something like, 'Come celebrate Halloween with us.' I was astounded! How could anyone use the house of God in such an abominable fashion?"

II Corinthians 6:15-17 reads: *And what concord hath Christ with Belial? or what part hath he that believeth with an infidel? And what agreement hath the temple of God with idols? for ye are the temple of the living God; as God hath said, I will dwell in them, and walk in them; and I will be their God, and they shall be my people. Wherefore come out from among them, and be ye separate.*

### "What Do I Do?"

You may ask the question, "What you say about Halloween, witches, haunted houses and ghosts may be true. But what do I do on October 31 when my children want to dress up in costume and scout the neighborhood in search of 'treats?' There's got to be an alternative . . . what is it?"

### Harvest Party

**An alternative to a Halloween Party might be to have a 'Harvest Party.'** Pastors, youth leaders or parents may plan this party where those who come might dress up like 'Bible characters' or some costume unrelated to the traditional Halloween. Another suggestion is to have a 'Country Party' where youths dress up in overalls and

HALLOWEEN Costumes

Western hats and scarves. This sort of 'Harvest Celebration' can be held around the time that Halloween is celebrated. It is much more sensible, and 'safer' than permitting children and youth to roam neighborhoods in darkness, having to fear such crazy things as 'apples with razor blades in them' or 'drug tainted candy.'

Parents may wish to have a *Prayer Meeting* during the time when the youths are having a party. This time of *intercession* should center around praying for the youth as well as 'rebuking Satan and the witches in the area.'

A great idea would be to have a 'Holy-ween' youth rally to bring other youths to a saving knowledge of Jesus Christ. What could be a more crushing blow to Satan than to have others won to Jesus on Satan's holiday!

**Halloween is not just fun and games. It is serious business. It is the time that witches celebrate more than any other time of year.**

If you have participated in the celebration of Halloween

(even as a child) we suggest you pray the following prayer renouncing any involvement in this or any other occult celebration:

"Lord Jesus, I renounce any involvement I have had with this pagan holiday, Halloween. I serve Satan notice that I will not be involved in the things that represent him, and I choose to do that which represents my Lord, Jesus Christ. Amen."

# 4

# "DABBLING"

In the Scriptures we are warned that the sins of the fathers are visited upon the third and fourth generations of those who disobey God.

*Thou shalt not bow down thyself to them, nor serve them: for I the Lord thy God am a jealous God, visiting the iniquity of the father upon the children unto the third and fourth generation of them that hate me.* Exodus 20:5

## The Occult

The word 'occult' comes from the Latin word, 'occultus' and it means things that are hidden, secret and mysterious.

Those who disregard God's warning and make contact with occult spirits risk certain terrible repercussions in the form of misery, sickness, insanity, and sometimes an early death.

Occult spirits are given ground in many ways. Unless the curse is broken, it will continue to plague the family and its descendants to the third and fourth generations. It predisposes people to be psychically oriented and sensitive; and through psychic heredity, to pick up more curses and spirits, thus extending the hereditary plague to forthcoming generations.

You may ask why do people who live in this enlightened age with all of its sophisticated science and technology still wish to get involved in occult practices?

One reason is, that in recent years there has been a denial of the cardinal doctrines of the Christian faith from those in a position of leadership in the church. Thus the parishioners, lacking spiritual food, have sought to fill that hunger in other ways.

Occult experiences, though deceptive, offer people a certain reality and answers for life's basic questions.

## Incantations
*There is an old and persistent belief that everything has a 'real' name, a name which enshrines the essence of the thing, which is the thing. Long ago, man learned that to know and pronounce the real name of a man or an animal is to experience power over it.*

*Words are weapons of power.* We use them to influence each other. Gestures and facial expressions help, but to communicate with clarity we usually use the tongue. Language is one of the great weapons of sorcery, and the magical use of words can be seen not only in the incantations of the 'Grimoires' but in many prayers. The Lord's Prayer has often been turned to magical uses. In the 13th century, Arnald of Villanova said that a priest cured him from over 100 warts in ten days. The priest touched each wart, made the sign of the cross and repeated The Lord's Prayer, but substituting for 'deliver us from evil' the words 'deliver Master Arnald from the wens and warts on his hands.' Then he took three stalks from a plant and put them in the ground in a damp and secluded place. When the stalks began to wither, the warts began to go. In time, the priest believed that the words of the prayer contained power which could be used for wart-charming.

In some of the Pueblo tribes in North America, the words of an incantation or a prayer must never be changed. In others, as in Europe, the magician may experiment with words and phrases until he hits on those which seem to work best for him. This respect is not confined to magicians as such. In 1963, The Ecumentical Council voted to authorize the saying of mass in languages other than Latin, provided that Latin was retained for 'The precise verbal formula which is essential to the sacrament', the words spoken by the priest, assuming the person of Christ and using the same ceremonies used by Christ as the Last Supper, which transform the bread and wine into the Body and Blood.

Incantations are one form of divination.

**You can be set free from Incantations!**

### Ouija Boards

The Dictionary of Mysticism gives this description of the Ouija Board:

> "An instrument for communication with the spirits of the dead. Made in various shapes and designs, some of them were used in the sixth century before Christ. The common feature of all its varieties is that an object moves under the hand of the medium, and one of its corners, or a pointer attached to it, spells out messages by successively pointing to letters of the alphabet marked on the board which is a part of the instrument."[1]

According to *The Ouija Board* by Edmond Gruss, devices like the Ouija board were known by the Chinese, Egyptians, Greeks and other ancient peoples. "In 1853, a French spiritist invented the *planchette,* described as a small heart-shaped table with three legs, one of which was actually a pencil. To operate it, one's fingers were placed on it and it was allowed to move over a piece of paper without conscious effort on the part of the operator."[2]

William Fuld of Baltimore has been credited with the invention of the Ouija board. However, it was patented by Elijah Bond in 1891. The common board as we know it today was patented on May 2, 1939. The Ouija board was very popular in the 1920's when it was reported that 3,000,000 boards had been sold. In the 1960's the revival of the occult brought along with it the increase in demand for the boards. Ownership of William Fuld, Inc. was purchased by Parker Brothers on February 23, 1966. And by the late 1970's sales were reported at 7,000,000 for the decade. "According to a nationwide survey taken by Stoker Hunt in 1983, more than 30 percent used the Ouija board to contact the dead and about the same number used it to contact the living."[3]

The instructions that come with the board say if you use it in a lighthearted way, asking silly questions and laughing over it, you'll get undeveloped influences around you.

**The Ouija board is NOT a game to play at a slumber party or a birthday party. It is a 'dead' serious 'occult' tool game. Nevertheless, there are people for whom the Ouija board is a religion. They consult it for guidance and live by what they learn from it. This is extremely dangerous and can lead to destruction.**

There are three basic explanations of why the Ouija board works. "The first view holds that inperceptible muscular movements cause the message indictor to move and the messages originate in the subconscious mind of the operator. The second view holds that much of what is communicated is subconscious, but a smaller portion derives from contact with disincarnate spirits. The third view is that much of what comes through the board comes from the subconscious mind of the operator, but a smaller portion reflects contact with evil spirits (demons)."[4] The third view is the view of Edmond Gruss and many Christians.

The messages are not always wicked or ungodly. Satan is a great deceiver. Deception is at the root of all Satanic acts (II Cor. 11:14; Rev. 12:9). There is the example of Mrs. John H. Curran from St. Louis, Missouri. She was able to write three novels, *The Sorry Tale, Hope Trueblood,* and *Telka* using the Ouija board. The novels contained accurate historical facts and a large percentage of Anglo-Saxon words, yet Mrs. Curran knew almost nothing about history nor had she traveled outside of her neighborhood.

Many people try to test the Ouija board. One such person was Sir William Barrett. He published his results in the September 1914 Proceedings of the American Society for Physical Research. His report implies that the board worked when the operators were blindfolded, when the alphabet was rearranged and when the board was covered up. Barrett stated in his book, *On the Threshold of the Unseen,* "Whatever may have been the source of the intelligence displayed, it was absolutely beyond the range of normal human faculty."[5]

Other strange Ouija board phenomena are: changes in the room temperature, strong winds in the room, the pointer moving by itself or messages given in foreign languages.

The Ouija board is a dangerous game. Dr. Carl Wickland, former director of the Psychopatic Institute of Chicago told that he was drawn into research of this when seemingly harmless experiences with the board led to insanity with several individuals.

There is also danger of possession. In *The Satan Trap,* Martin Ebon states, "It is significant, however, that the greatest outcry against Ouijas has come from the spiritualists — not the parapsychologists. In England, spiritualists groups are petitioning to ban the sale of Ouijas as toys for children — not because of vague dangers of 'unhealthy effects or naive suggestible persons' — but because they fear the children will become possessed."[6]

No one knows how many murders have been caused that relate somehow to the Ouija board. Ernest Turley was shot and killed by his 15 year-old daughter. In her testimony she explained, "that in a Ouija board seance with her mother the board told her to kill her father so her mother . . . 'could marry a young cowboy . . .'"[7]

In the book *Fads, Follies and Delusions of the American People,* Paul Sann describes another incident. Herbert Hurd killed his wife because the Ouija board had lied to her. The board had said that he was too fond of another woman and that he had given the woman a large sum of money. Mr. Hurd was unable to convince his wife of the truth and that the Ouija board was wrong, so he killed her.

In Florida the headline read: **"Miami School Hysteria Linked to Ouija Board."**[8] The story went on to say that classes were back to normal after an outbreak of hysteria caused by hypnosis and the Ouija board. The teacher of the class said, "'an Ouija board game had gotten out of control . . . 'Everybody just got carried away and it was a riot . . . There were girls screaming that there was a spirit inside the board.'"[9]

There is also a lot of direct denial of the Christian faith. In any messages recorded from a wide variety of people, "there is omission if not denial of sin, the Trinity, the Resurrection, Judgement Day, and so on."[10]

According to Gina Covina in her book *The Ouija Book,* voices say we are all gods, the Ouija is a tool to become more like a god, or even become god. This gives an erroneous view to the ultimate meaning of man's existance.

The Bible contains many references to various forms of divination and all are explicitly forbidden for the believer. (See Chapter Five.)

**You can be set free from the Ouija board!**

### Dungeons and Dragons

*Dungeons and Dragons* is a game which opens its players up to Satan. There are many parents, educators, and even some pastors who do not see the evil in this game which has its roots in fantasy, torture, witchcraft and warfare.

*Dungeons and Dragons,* commonly referred to as *D & D,* is a fantasy game in which each player assumes the identity of the character he creates. In this game, the 'creature' that the player creates is based on the chance roll of the dice. *D & D is the most popular of war and mystical fantasy games available. Instead of fighting on historical battlefields, battles are fought in the players' minds. The Dungeon Master* (DM), often seen as a god, sets the stage in the fantasy world. The participants step into medieval personalities who journey through incredible adventures so far as they want. There is no set ending to *D & D* and other fantasy role-playing games. Instead, the only limit to the game is the players' imaginations. For those with particularly vivid imaginations, the game can become an almost mystical experience, consuming, addictive, and potentially dangerous. In fact, there are many documented cases where a group of people played the same game for several years.

The object of *D & D,* designed for three or more players age ten and up, is to maneuver the characters through a maze of dungeons (tunnels) filled with monsters, magic, ambushes, and adventures in search of treasures. Each character has six basic abilities, determined by the roll of the dice: strength, intelligence, wisdom, constitution, dexterity and charisma. Also, each character is equipped with special aids to survive the journeys through the dungeons: magical weapons, potions, spells and magical trinkets, such as holy water, garlic and wolves-bane. They are also given more conventional weapons including daggers, hand axes, swords and battle axes. Each player can stay in the game so long as his character is not killed, thus leaving open the possibility for the game to continue for years. However, *the longer the game continues, the more likely the players will identify themselves with the character, causing the line between reality and fantasy to grow 'fuzzy.'*

D & D is known to cause D & D players to lose the difference between reality and fiction. According to the *Pentecostal Evangel, D & D* also has been responsible for over 90 deaths in young people. Dr. Thomas Radecki, chairman of the National Coalition for Television Violence (NCTV) and psychiatrist at the University of Illinois, states that the evidence is overwhelming that heavy participation in D & D has caused several dozens of murders and suicides. "'When you really delve into it and go and talk to these people in jail cells, the evidence is overwhelming' he said of the trials he has been involved with. 'Without D & D, the crimes would not have occurred — there's not the slightest doubt in my mind.'"[11]

Radecki is also alarmed not only with the deaths that are connected to D & D, but also its link to Satanic worship. He feels certain that the epidemiological research evidence is clear that becoming involved with D & D can lead many players into deep involvement with the occult and Satan worship. Tens of thousands are becoming involved, says Radecki, and worship of violence can lead to family abuse and abuse of others outside of the home.

According to Radecki, D & D includes many descriptions of killing, including human sacrifice, assassination, sadism, premeditated murder and curses of insanity. One mother of a D & D victim said that much of the material comes from demonology including witchcraft and evil monsters. She went on to say that the game details multiple curses of insanity including suicidal and homicidal mania. The *Dungeon Master's Guide* notes that suicidal mania is a type of insanity that causes the affected person to have incredible urges to destroy himself or herself whenever the means are made possible. It is very clear that people without any health problems can be harmed by *D & D*. The problem is not that emotional people are playing this game, but that people are playing it.

NCTV, along with *Bothered About D & D* group (BADD), keep track of *D & D*-related deaths and have lobbied against the game. In 1986, BADD was successful in helping to get the Saturday morning cartoon off the air. However, little other success has been made. Both NCTV and BADD have tried to get the U.S. Federal Trade Commission, the Consumer Safety Products Commission and the White House involved but with no luck. In the meantime, Radecki predicts that the number of *D & D* deaths will increase and there are probably many *D & D*-related deaths that NCTV or BADD will never hear about.

In my book, *Turmoil In The Toy Box,* I quote, "Fantasies, in and of themselves, serve a healthy function, like relieving boredom,"[12] says Michigan psychologist Dr. Jack McGaugh. "Like any good thing, it can be over done. What you think about, you become at the time."[13] Another Michigan psychologist, Dr. Douglas Brown, believes the same. "Life for most people is boring. There's not much excitement. We've run out of frontiers. The only frontiers we have left are in our minds. Testing yourself becomes the challenge."[14] He does offer one caution, however. "If a person isn't too well put together to begin with, it's not going to be good for him."[15]

I do not agree with the above statement:

**Statement:** "Fantasies, in and of themselves, serve a healthy function, like relieving boredom."
**Objection:** The more we fantasize on something, the more likely we are to bring that fantasy to reality through our actions. This can be either good or bad.

**Statement:** "The only frontier we have left is in our minds."

**Objection:** God gives us thoughts. The only true way we can expand our creative thinking is to establish and cultivate our relationship with God.

The game's creator, Gary Gygax, admits that *D & D* players are fervid followers. "They ARE dedicated. They get really caught up in it. But I've met some obsessed golfers and tennis players, too. *Dungeons and Dragons* is just a different kind of release."[16]

Despite the game's skyrocketing popularity, many people, both Christian and non-Christian, are expressing concerns over the harmful effects the game is having on today's youth. According to Dr. Gary North, author of *None Dare Call It Witchcraft*, " . . . after years of study of the history of occultism, after having researched a book on the subject, and after having consulted with scholars in the field of historical research, I can say with confidence: these games are the most effective, most magnificently packaged, most profitably marketed, and most thoroughly researched introduction to the occult in man's recorded history."[17]

Some examples of blasphemy are found in quotes taken from the more than 20 books that teach one how to play *Dungeons and Dragons:*

### Concerning 'Deities' and 'Gods'

"This game lets all your fantasies come true. This is a world where monsters, dragons, good and evil; high priests, fierce demons; and even the gods themselves may enter your character's life."[18]

In other sections the gods are referrred to as 'deity':
(1) "It is well known by all experienced players . . . spells bestowed upon them by their respective deities.
(2) "Each cleric must have his or her own deity.
(3) "The deity (you the DM 'Dungeon Master') will point out all the transgressions . . ."[19]

"Serving a deity is a significant part of *D & D,* and all player characters should have a patron god. Alignment assumes its full importance when tied to the worship of a deity."[20]

"Changing alignment: Whether or not the character actively professes some deity, he or she will have an alignment and serve one or more deities of this general alignment indirectly or unbeknownst to the character."[21]

### Concerning Prayer and Fasting
"Clerical spells . . . are bestowed by the gods, so that the cleric need but pray for a few hours . . ."[22]

Cleric desires third through fifth level spells, the monions (angels, demigods, or whatever) will be likely to require the cleric to spend two to eight days in prayer, fasting, and contemplation of his or her transgressions, making whatever sacrifices and atonement are necessary . . . Spell recovery . . . requires about the same period of time in order to pray and meditate . . ."[23]

### Concerning Magic and Spells
"Swords and sorcery best describe what this game is all about . . . so mind unleashing, that it comes near reality.

"Most spells have a verbal component and so must be uttered."[24]

"The spell caster should be required to show you what form of protective inscription he or she has used when the spell is cast. The three forms mentioned are: Pictures of a magic circle, pentagram, and thaumaturgic triangle."[25] According to experts in witchcraft and Satanic worship.

### Concerning Clerics
"Another important attribute of the cleric is the ability to turn away (or actually command into service) the undead and less powerful demons and devils."[26]

### Concerning Death
'Resurrection' is referred to as "the revival of a character after its death by magical means."[27]

### Concerning Satanism
"'Elric (hero)' — the sign being given by his left hand (which is called the Goat Head sign) means 'Satan is lord' to all Satan worshippers."[28]

The word 'demon' appears 106 times in pages 16-19 of the

*Monster Manual.* And the player has been told to trust four of these demons as (lesser gods) on page 105, paragraph 5, of the *Deities and Demigods* book.

The word 'devil' appears 94 times and the word 'hell' appears 25 times in pages 20-23 of the *Monster Manual.*

### Concerning Defilement
**In the following excerpt from page 115 of the** *Players Handbook,* blesses and curses, and unholy and holy are treated as equals.

"Defilement of Fonts: If any non-believer blesses/curses an unholy/holy font, or uses less refined means such as excreting wastes into a font or basin, the whole is absolutely desecrated, defiled, and unfit . . . Note that either method of defilement requires actual contact with the font and its vessel. Any blessing or cursing from a distance will be absolutely ineffectual and wasted."[29]

The above practices that the game employs and forces the player to do likewise are indeed the exact practices that God forbids in the Bible. Still many Christians say, "I'm a Christian, and I play *D & D.*" And others contend that the game is just fantasy, that they would never do these things in real life. In the *New Testament,* Christ teaches that fantasy can be evil. *But I say unto you, That whosoever looketh on a woman to lust after her, he hath committed adultery with her already in his heart* (Matthew 5:28).
**You can be set free from *Dungeons & Dragons!***

### Tarot Cards
Tarot cards are usually regarded as a system of fortune telling using a special pack of fancy cards. It can be described as "the cosmic method in universal creation or emanation, including its purpose and result."[30] It is generally associated with the *Tree Of Life of the Cabala* but it also has connection to the pyramids of Egypt and with Indian theosophical philosophy. However, Tarot cards can also be paired as

opposites or complementaries. They can also be arranged in a circle to suggest the universe.

According to occult tradition, the Tarot pack forms a complete symbolic system. Different packs use varying designs and symbols, but there is a rough general similarity. The pack has four suits — *Wands, Cups, Swords* and *Pentacles* — of 14 cards each, plus 22 extra cards called trumps or *Major Arcana*.

rises.
he origins of the Tarot are not clearly ned. A. E. Waite concluded that it had exoteric history before the 14th century the oldest examples of Tarot cards bably date from about 1390, while occult ilition places their origin at about 0 AD. It is said that the gypsies are

spoken of the written word
The four suits are designated Wands, Cups, Swords and Pentacles, symbolizing amongst other things fire, water, air and earth: in each suit are four court cards: the King, the essential Self, 'Spirit', in man; the Queen, the 'Soul' or inner pattern part of a particular human personality; the Knight.

According to occult tradition, the pack was invented by adepts and forms a plete symbolic system. Different packs varying designs and symbols, but there rough general similarity. The pack has suits — Wands, Cups, Swords and Penti (below) — of 14 cards each, plus 22 cards called trumps or Major Arcana

ACE OF WANDS. ACE OF CUPS. ACE OF SWORDS. ACE OF PENTACL

Tarot Cards

There are no standard pictures on the cards. Usually the pictures are crude and not very well drawn. "The four suits designated Wands, Cups, Swords, and Pentacles, symbolize amongst other things fire, water, air and earth: in each suit are four court cards: the *King*, the essential self, 'Spirit', in man; the *Queen*, the 'Soul' or inner pattern part of a particular human personality; the *Knight*, representing the special focusing of energies and a persons sense of selfhood; the

*Page* or *Esquire,* standing for the Body or personal vehicle."[31] The Tarot card numbered *13* is Death, the skeleton.

The origin of Tarot cards is not clearly defined but is believed to have begun after the 14th century, probably from about 1390. Gypsies are believed to hold the first set of cards and they alone know the secret of its meaning.

The Tarot in its cabalistic form sets out to show the relation between God, Man and the Universe; among other things it is a symbol of incarnation. Tarot cards try to recall symbols, meanings and correspondence to the cards from the person's subconscious mind. By means of suggestion they try to reveal the truth hidden in our consciousness. Most people are not concerned with the suits of the cards but with the trumps or Major Arcana, since they believe these cards control their destiny or future. There are many interpretations to the cards because there are so many interpreters.

**You can be set free from Tarot Cards!**

### Tea-Leaf Reading

Although telling fortunes by consulting the patterns formed by tea-leaves on the base and sides of a cup is often considered entertainment, it is not just an amusement. The tea-leaves can act as a medium through which the clairvoyance of the reader is stimulated so that he or she is able to reveal truth that would otherwise remain hidden; or the figures formed by the leaves may be believed to reflect patterns that exist in the astral.

The method of tea-leaf reading is simple: The client inverts his cup, turning it around three times; he places it on the saucer and then taps the bottom three time with his left index finger. The *clairvoyant,* who is in a light trance, picks the cup up and turns it around so that the leaves can be inspected. The interpretation of the patterns might indicate that the client will take a journey, have a child or children, a love affair, and so on.

**You can be set free from Tea-Leaf Reading!**

## Scrying

*Scrying means seeing* — or seeing into the future. This is a kind of divination which uses 'transparent' materials such as water, crystals, mirrors, in which are formed visions of the future.

In our time the most popular form of scrying is that which uses the crystal ball — *crystal-gazing*. From the primitive tribes of north Borneo to today, crystal has been used to *reveal* the future.

Since sitting and staring into a glass ball is a lot less work than drawing up horoscopes or laying out Tarot cards, this form of divination has been popular throughout the centuries. Crystal-gazers can be found wherever back-street fortune tellers think a living can be made.

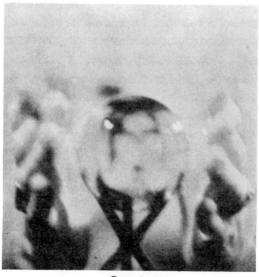

Scrying

75

Most crystal-gazers say that the crystal seems to become foggy and opaque from the inside, and then the mists clear away to reveal a vision which may range from swirling, abstract shapes to clearcut scenes from reality.

Crystal is also used in many other ways. Quartz crystal, silicon dioxide, now has more uses than a Veg-O-Matic. One woman puts a crystal next to her carburetor to keep her car running smoothly. Another woman drops a crystal into her moisturizer to improve her skin. It is reported that another person cures common sicknesses by drinking water that had crystals soaking in it over night.

*People Magazine* reports that Tina Turner finds that holding a crystal for a few moments takes away the loneliness of a strange hotel room. Nationwide, crystal prices and sales have more than tripled after Shirley MacLaine brought spiritualism and healing to prime time television.

According to one West Coast crystal consultant, crystals should be used as tools to bring out your own 'spiritual' gifts. This consultant says you must be careful to choose the proper tool for the job — ". . . amethyst, historically thought to cure drunkeness, also protects the respiratory system and promotes healing if placed on the body's pressure points. Rose quartz affects matters of the heart, smoky quartz the nerves, while tourmaline balances mental and emotional states and has a direct line to the intestinal system."[32]

It is stated that crystals must first be cleared by passing them through sand or sea salt or exposing them to sunshine or moonlight. Then the owner must 'charge' the crystal by blowing on it with a wish to give it a special purpose.

In history, nobility draped themselves with crystals to ward off the Plague. When Pope Clement VII got sick, they had him eat crushed gemstones. (He died soon after.) Today crystals are used in radios, lazers, computers and watches because of their ability to vibrate in response to electricity.

Many people are trying to make money from the new awareness on crystals. One company in California says as long as you are in unity and peace with yourself, you can eat what you want and not gain weight. Two entrepreneurs are going to sell 21 types of crystals, for $20-$100. The crystals will have their own pedigree and a booklet explaining their uses and origin. Another company in New York City is organizing trips to Arkansas, "so you can find your own crystal."

According to Dr. Gershon Lesser, an L.A. internist, there is no scientific basis that stones can heal. However, he states that if the stone creates a belief system then it can be a help to the body. He feels the meditation involved does help the person.

**Any method of scrying is an ABOMINATION in the eyes of God, for He has said in Exodus 15:27: "... for I am the Lord that healeth thee."**

**You can be set free from Scrying!**

### The Third Eye

An eye shown in some abnormal position on the body stands for supernatural sight, clairvoyance and power. According to the Hindus each man has a hidden third eye, which is in the middle of the forehead just above the point where the eyebrows meet.

Conversely, the one-eyed Cyclops of Greek mythology, a creature with less than the proper complement of eyes, is likely to have subnormal vision and wisdom.

**You can be set free from the Third Eye!**

Observe the THIRD Eye

### Talismans

The word *Talisman* is defined in the *Oxford English Dictionary* as an "object engraven with figures or characters to which are attributed the occult powers of the planetary influences and celestrial configurations under which it was made; usually worn as an amulet to avert evil or bring fortune to the wearer."[33] Talismans are objects believed to attract favorable influences like these tokens.

All races have traditional amulets. In ancient Egypt, the land where there was an abundance of wearers of the amulet, they were worn by the living and placed in the inner coffin of the mummy; the Chinese carry an object engraved with a character from the ancient text, the Shu-Ching; the Jew fastens at his door a little roll of parchment inscribed with Shadai; the Mohammedan uses a verse from the Koran. Anything from natural objects to jewels like garnets and jade, to berries, animals' hair and the rabbit's foot are used as talismans. Coral, especially the red or pink variety, was used with bells on babies rattles mainly because it was believed to safeguard against the Evil Eye, which was a primitive and ancient fear of being watched by an enemy. (The Evil Eye took two distinct forms, the one voluntary, which was inspired by malice, and the other involuntary, over which the 'unlucky' person had no control.)

Down through the ages talismans have been used for 'healing.' Satan is a counterfeiter and this is one way he attempts to copy the miracles of Christ and his diciples. Do not be deceived. The word 'talisman' has no relationship to the miracles of Christ and his disciples.

**You can be set free from Talismans!**

### Palmistry

The belief that man's destiny is imprinted on his hand has a long history. For centuries it is argued that an accurate interpretation of the configurations of the hand can enable a man to recognize and change his fate. The tradition that every line, star, point, cross, square, island and triangle in the hand is significant has been passed on from generation to generation. Likewise, the palmist of today believes that there is a relationship between physical features and man's nature.

The occultist says that there is a constant interplay, not only between the physical and the mental, but also between these and the spiritual. The palmist believes, in addition to that mentioned above, that the past and the future may be read.

Palmistry

God does not work through 'palmistry' or any other form of *fortune-telling*. This, too, is an ABOMINATION in the sight of God.
**You can be set free from Palmistry!**

### Necromancy

Probably the most black of the 'black arts' is *necromancy*, communication with the dead. Necromancy can be divided into two main branches: divination by means of ghosts, and divination from corpses, both which represent related forms of forbidden knowledge.

According to the Biblical story of Saul and the 'witch' of Endor, the king failed to obtain an omen of the future from God, by dreams, or by lots, or by prophets, and consulted a

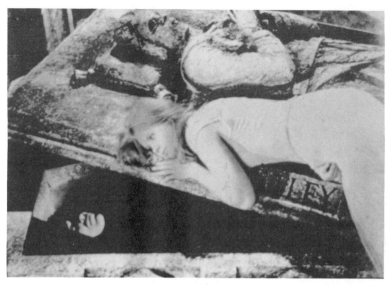

Necromancy

medium who summoned up for him the shape of the prophet Samuel. The ghost appeared as an old man dressed in a robe, and foretold Saul's imminent death and the defeat of Israel. I Samuel, Chapter 28.

**You can be set free from Necromancy!**

## Ritual Magic

Magical textbooks, called *Grimoires* contain all sorts of processes, including instructions for making love talismans or wax images. One ceremony is to summon up a 'spirit', supernatural force or entity of some kind which can be overpowered by the magician and forced to carry out his orders or reveal what it knows.

A secluded place should be chosen for the ceremony so as to avoid interruptions. Graveyards, ruins, crossroads or dark woods are suitable for destructive magic and communing with evil spirits. If the ceremony is performed indoors, all

Magic

the windows and doors should be closed; and the room should be hung with drapes of a color appropriate to the planet, instructs this book of magic.

**You can be set free from Ritual Magic!**

### Edgar Cayce

Edgar Cayce of Hopkinsville, Kentucky, known as 'the Man of Miracles' who died in 1945, was an occult miracle worker who held a prominent place in the field of unorthodox medicine. With very little formal training, *Edgar Cayce became a 'doctor' when in a trance state, and treated some 30,000 patients before his death in 1945.*

Cayce became aware of his power of healing when he was 16 years old. Hit in the back by a baseball, he ordered his mother to apply a poultice and by morning he was cured — yet he could remember nothing of what had taken place.

Later, he sought the advice of a hypnotist for healing of his throat.

Edgar Cayce soon became well known and many sick people who doctors had given up on came to him from all over the country. He began to diagnose illnesses and prescribe cures for many people. Invariably, Cayce went into a trance and started with the words "Yes, we see the body."[34] A hospital was established in Virginia Beach, Virginia to accomodate the crowds of people who were coming to him for help. In 1931, the foundation, the *Association of Research and Enlightenment,* was formed. Cayce's son, Hugh Lynn, became leader of the organization after his father's death.

Not only was he a psychic healer, he also used much 'backwoods' therapy like bed bug juice or oil of smoke. He also was clairvoyant and at one time was used to solve a murder case. In some of his trances he could also predict the future.

"Like many others in the field of fringe medicine, Cayce created his own occult philosophy, much of which had developed from questions submitted to him while under a trance state. His philosophy seemed to combine many of the elements of Theosophy, Christianity, and Pyramidology, no doubt the result of Cayce's extensive reading in his youth."[35]

How sad that this man did not follow the truth of the Word of God.

**You can be set free from Edgar Cayce!**

### Rosicrucians

Rosicrucians were believed to be members of a German mystical or occult order that suddenly became active during the second decade of the 17th century, however, they are said to trace their origins back to the early part of the 15th century.

Vaudeville Show Advertisement

It is believed that the Rosicrucians possessed important and arcane wisdom that had been inherited by them and passed on to their spiritual heirs and successors. They were called 'Brethren of the Rosy C.' The legend began with the story of Christian Rosenkreuz's travels in search of knowledge and true wisdom and ended with the formation of the Rosicrucians. Rosenkreuz, a former monk, enlisted the services of three monks from his old monastery to join him as disciples and helpers. The Fratres (Brothers) pledged themselves to keep secret all that they learned from him, but to record everything in a manuscript book for the benefit of their successors.

One of the most interesting features of the Rosicrucian legend is the persistence with which it has survived, particularly in circles identified with occultism. The mythical Christian Rosenkreuz (literally 'Rosy Cross') represents a forerunner of the 'Secret Chiefs' who added lustre to Baron von Hund's *Masonic Rite of the Strict Observance* (Germany, late 18th century). Legend has it that they never existed, but many people believed in them.

**You can be set free from Rosicrucians and other secret societies!**

### Good Luck Charms

Good luck charms, the Egyptian *ankh* (a cross with a loop at the top which was an ancient fertility symbol), the ancient witchcraft sign of the broken cross (popularly known as the peace symbol), a wiggley tail which is called the 'Italian Horn' (Cornu), astrological symbols and other jewelry with hex signs can have ill effects on someone seeking deliverance from the occult. Amulets are said to guard against the third or 'Evil Eye.' Some objects, particularly rings, bracelets and other jewelry, which has been given to a person by someone who is involved in witchcraft, will have bondages and/or curses in them, . . . and on and on.

**You can be set free from Good Luck Charms!**

### Pentagram

The five-pointed star, used for centuries by witches, is called the *pentacle,* or *pentagram.* With the two points up (as in Eastern Star) it is called the sign of the goat or Satan.

One point up symbolizes witchcraft.

SATANIC STAR
(Pentagram)

Turn goat's head star upside down to observe another face.

When witches want to talk to demons they often will stand within a pentagram. Then the demon will appear within a hexagram, a six-pointed star formed by two triangles. The hexagram is a Cabalistic magic symbol for white magic. The word hex comes from the word hexagram. Some farmers of the Pennsylvania Dutch country will put hex signs on their barns to ward off witches all throughout the year. We are so innocently deceived by symbols of witchcraft. Gift shops have the 'kitchen witch', hex signs, magic tricks and more.

**You can be set free from the Pentagram!**

## Hex Signs

From the time of the first century Christian church, and even before this, numbers, animals, geometric designs and colors have had an 'extra-ordinary' significance. Images carved on the walls of the cave dwellers; especially those found in Europe spell out the truth of this statement. Crude circles filled with color and depicting periods of life were found throughout the caves. Primitive man used these 'circle signs' to possibly appease the gods or frighten off intruders. Throughout the centuries these signs, which held secret meanings, were used to ward off evil spirits, spells and disease. Even today, the Hex Sign can be found on the barns and in the homes of some Pennsylvania Dutch people.

## Symbols of the Hex Signs

(1) **Love and Marriage**—Double good luck and lots of love.

(2) **The Irish Shamrock Hex**—Good Luck, Easy Life, Good Fortune, Fidelity.

(3) **Power**—Ultimate triumph over evil.

(4) **Unicorn**—Virtue and Piety.

(5) **Fertility**—Make fruitful or productive.

(6) **Twelve Petal Rosette**—That each month of the year be a joyous one.

(7) **The Distelfink**—The Bird of Happiness always near you. Good fortune.

(8) **Your Lucky Stars**—Lucky stars that guide your heart.

(9) **Love and Romance**—Rosette and hearts of love and romance.

(10) **Eight-Pointed Star**—Star and rosette to bring abundance and goodwill.

(11) **Welcome**—Good luck and Welcome.

(12) **Friendship.**[36]

**You can be set free from the Hex Sign!**

(1)

(2)

(3)

(4)

(5)

(6)

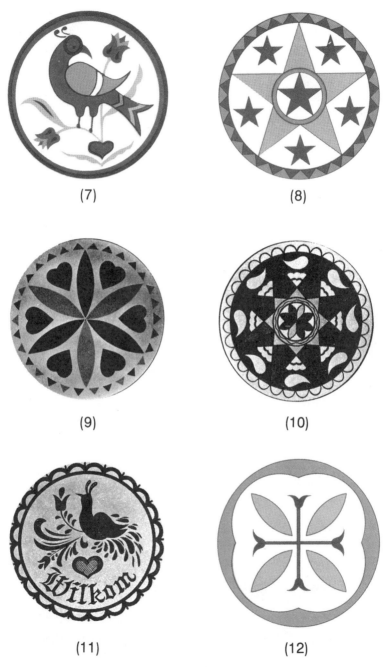

(7)

(8)

(9)

(10)

(11)

(12)

# 5

# TWELVE FORBIDDEN PRACTICES

### 1. Enchantments
The act of influencing by charms and incantations the practice of magical arts.

Deuteronomy 18:10
Exodus 7:11,22; 8:7
Numbers 23:23; 24:1
Leviticus 19:26
II Kings 17:17; 21:6
II Chronicles 33:6
Ecclesiastes 10:11
Isaiah 47:9,12
Jeremiah 27:9
Exodus 7:11,22:

*Then Pharaoh also called the wise men and the sorcerers: now the magicians of Egypt, they also did in like manner with their enchantments. And the magicians of Egypt did so with their enchantments: and Pharoah's heart was hardened, neither did he hearken unto them; as the Lord hath said.*

Exodus 8:7:

*And the magicians did so with their enchantments, and brought up frogs upon the land of Egypt.*

II Chronicles 33:6:

*And he caused his children to pass through the fire in the valley of the son of Hinnom: also he observed times, and used enchantments, and used witchcraft, and dealt with a familiar spirit, and with wizards: he wrought much evil in the sight of the Lord, to provoke him to anger.*

Jeremiah 27:9:

*Therefore hearken not ye to your prophets, nor to your diviners, nor to your dreamers, nor to your enchanters, nor to your sorcerers, which speak unto you, saying, Ye shall not serve the king of Babylon:*

Leviticus 19:26:

*Ye shall not eat any thing with the blood: neither shall ye use enchantment, nor observe times*

### Enchanter

Sorcerer, magician, one who uses the human voice or music to bring another person under psychic control.

Leviticus 19:26

Deuteronomy 18:10-12

II Chronicles 33:6

II Kings 17:17

Isaiah 47:8-11

Jeremiah 27:9

Daniel 1:20

Deuteronomy 18:10-12:

*There shall not be found among you any one that maketh his son or his daughter to pass through the fire, or that useth divination, or an observer of times, or an enchanter, or a witch, Or a charmer, or a consulter with familiar spirits, or a wizard, or a necromancer. For all that do these things are an abomination unto the Lord: and because of these abominations the Lord thy God doth drive them out from before thee.*

Daniel 1:20:

*And in all matters of wisdom and understanding, that the king inquired of them, he found them ten times better than*

*all the magicians and astrologers that were in all his realm.*
II Kings 17:17:
*And they caused their sons and their daughters to pass through the fire, and used divination and enchantments, and sold themselves to do evil in the sight of the Lord, to provoke him to anger.*

## 2. **Witchcraft**

The practice of dealing with evil spirits, the use of sorcery or magic.

Exodus 22:18
Deuteronomy 18:10-12
I Samuel 15:23
II Kings 9:22
II Chronicles 33:6
Micah 5:12
Nahum 3:4
Galatians 5:19-21
I Samuel 15:23:
*For rebellion is as the sin of witchcraft, and stubbornness is as iniquity and idolatry. Because thou hast rejected the word of the Lord, he hath also rejected thee from being king.*
Exodus 22:18:
*Thou shalt not suffer a witch to live.*
Micah 5:12:
*And I will cut off witchcrafts out of thine hand; and thou shalt have no more soothsayers:*
Galatians 5:19-21:
*Now the works of the flesh are manifest, which are these; Adultery, fornication, uncleanness, lasciviousness, Idolatry, witchcraft, hatred, variance, emulations, wrath, strife, seditions, heresies, Envyings, murders, drunkenness, revellings, and such like: of the which I tell you before, as I have also told you in time past, that they which do such*

things shall not inherit the kingdom of God.

3. **Sorcery** (Pharmaika)

The use of power gained from the assistance or control of evil spirits, especially for divining.

Exodus 7:11
Isaiah 47:9,12; 57:3
Jeremiah 27:9
Daniel 2:2
Malachi 3:5
Revelation 9:21; 18:23; 21:8; 22:15

Malachi 3:5:

And I will come near to you to judgement; and I will be a swift witness against the sorcerers, and against the adulterers, and against false swearers, and against those that oppress the hireling in his wages, the widow, and the fatherless, and that turn aside the stranger from his right, and fear not me, saith the Lord of hosts.

Revelation 21:8:

But the fearful, and unbelieving, and the abominable, and murderers, and whoremongers, and sorcerers, and idolaters, and all liars, shall have their part in the lake which burneth with fire and brimstone: which is the second death.

4. **Divination**

Fortune-telling
Numbers 22:7
II Kings 18:10-14
Jeremiah 27:8-9
Jeremiah 29:8-9
Acts 16:16-24

Jeremiah 29:8-9:

For thus saith the Lord of hosts, the God of Israel; Let not your prophets and your diviners, that be in the midst of you, deceive you, neither hearken to your dreams which ye *caused to be dreamed. For they prophesy falsely unto you in my name: I have not sent them, saith the Lord.*

5. **Wizardry**

The art of practices of a wizard; sorcery.

**Wizard**

One skilled in magic; sorcerer; male witch (to destroy in Israel).

Exodus 22:18

Leviticus 19:31; 20:6, 27

Deuteronomy 18:11

II Kings 17:17

II Kings 21:6, 23:24

II Chronicles 33:6

Isaiah 8:19; 19:3

Leviticus 19:31:

*Regard not them that have familiar spirits, neither seek after wizards, to be defiled by them: I am the Lord your God.*

Leviticus 20:27:

*A man also or a woman that hath a familar spirit, or that is a wizard, shall surely be put to death: they shall stone them with stones: their blood shall be upon them.*

II Kings 23:24:

*Moreover the workers with familiar spirits, and the wizards, and the images, and the idols, and all the abominations that were spied in the land of Judah and Jerusalem, did Josiah put away, that he might perform the words of the law which were written in the book that Hilkiah the priest found in the house of the Lord.*

6. **Necromancy**

Communication with the dead; conjuration of the spirits of the dead for purposes of magically revealing the future or influencing the course of events.

Deuteronomy 18:11

I Samuel 28:1-25
Isaiah 8:19
I Chronicles 10:13-14
Isaiah 8:19:
*And when they shall say unto you, Seek unto them that have familiar spirits, and unto wizards that peep, and that mutter: should not a people seek unto their God? for the living to the dead?*

7. **Charm**
Put a spell upon someone; to affect by magic.
Deuteronomy 18:11
Isaiah 19:3
Isaiah 19:3:
*And the spirit of Egypt shall fail in the midst therof; and I will destroy the counsel thereof: and they shall seek unto the idols, and to the charmers, and to them that have familiar spirits, and to the wizards.*

8. **Star Gazing/Astrology**
The divination of the supposed influence of the stars upon human affairs and terrestrial events by their positions and aspects.
Isaiah 47:12-15
Jeremiah 10:2
Daniel 1:18-20
Daniel 2:1-49
Daniel 4:1-37
Daniel 5:7-15
Jeremiah 10:2:
*Thus saith the Lord, Learn not the way of the heathen, and be not dismayed at the signs of heaven; for the heathen are dismayed at them.*

9. **Soothsaying**
The act of foretelling events; prophesying by a spirit other than the Holy Spirit.

Joshua 13:22
Micah 5:12-15
Acts 16:16-18
Micah 5:12-15:

*And I will cut off witchcrafts out of thine hand; and thou shalt have no more soothsayers: Thy graven images also will I cut off, and thy standing images out of the midst of thee; and thou shalt no more worship the work of thine hands. And I will pluck up thy groves out of the midst of thee; so will I destroy thy cities. And I will execute vengeance in anger and fury upon the heathen, such as they have not heard.*

## 10. Prognostication

To foretell from signs or symptoms; prophesying without the Holy Spirit; soothsaying.

Isaiah 47:12-15
Joshua 13:22
Micah 5:12-15
Acts 16:16-18
Isaiah 47:12-15:

*Stand now with thine enchantments, and with the multitude of thy sorceries, wherein thou hast laboured from thy youth; if so be thou shalt be able to profit, if so be thou mayest prevail. Thou art wearied in the multitude of thy counsels. Let now the astrologers, the stargazers, the monthly prognosticators, stand up, and save thee from these things that shall come upon thee. Behold, they shall be as stubble; the fire shall burn them; they shall not deliver themselves from the power of the flame: there shall not be a coal to warm at, not a fire to sit before it. Thus shall they be unto thee with whom thou has laboured, even thy merchants, from thy youth: they shall wander every one to his quarter; none shall save thee.*

## 11. Observing Times
Astrology.
Leviticus 19:26
Deuteronomy 18:10-14
II Kings 21:6
II Chronicles 33:6
II Kings 21:6:
*And he made his son pass through the fire, and observed times, and used enchantments, and dealt with familiar spirits and wizards: he wrought much wickedness in the sight of the Lord, to provoke him to anger.*

## 12. Magic
Witchcraft.
Deuteronomy 18:10-12
II Chronicles 33:6
I Samuel 15:23
Deuteronomy 18:10-12:
*There shall not be found among you any one that maketh his son or his daughter to pass through fire, or that useth divination, or an observer of times, or an enchanter, or a witch, Or a charmer, or a consulter with familiar spirits, or a wizard, or a necromancer. For all that do these things are an abomination unto the Lord: and because of these abominations the Lord thy God doth drive them out from before thee.*

# 6

# SATAN IS ALIVE AND WELL

Matthew 10:28 warns: *And fear not them which kill the body, but are not able to kill the soul: but rather fear him which is able to destroy both the soul and body in hell.*

### Witches

The name *witch* comes from the Saxon word *wica*, meaning 'wise one.' *Wicca* is the feminine form of an old English word, *wicca*, meaning witch and has worship as its main object. The additional element of magic lends to the cult of witchcraft an illicit and undoubtedly attractive aura. Wicca is primarily a fertility religion, strongly influenced by the theory of the late Margaret Murray that medieval witchraft was a survival of the pagan fertility religion of pre-Christian Europe.

Both male and female members of Wicca are known as witches, although the cult is mainly matriarchal, with a high priestess being likened to that of deity of witchlore. To some degree she is likened to the Virgin Mary of Roman Catholicism; she is Queen of Heaven, and her symbols are the moon and stars. She is light, love and above all fertility. Her consort, personified by the high priest, is the horned god — Cernunnos, Pan, Osiris.

### The Witches' Brew

Witches stirring a brew in a large cooking pot is another

symbol of Halloween. Often, witches were seen on country roads carrying bundles of food and large cooking cauldrons. Once at their meeting place, they would gather firewood, herbs, and fruits. After finding water they would take three good-sized green branches with which they fashioned a tripod to hold the cauldron. When the broth flavored with herbs and berries began to bubble they would roast horse-flesh, sacred to pagan gods, over the hot coals.

Witches at Caldron-Demons

The story goes that travelers who passed by reported seeing the witches peer into their cauldrons, cackling and smacking their lips as the firelight gave their weird faces an eerie glow.

It is widely known that people who practiced witchcraft really did concoct such mixtures for casting spells, and women who were not witches brewed cauldrons of herbs to cure headaches, backaches, fevers and colds. It behoved any old woman to be careful not to talk to herself while stirring her brew lest she be accused of being a witch:

> Fillet of a fenny snake,
> In the caldron boil and bake;
> Eye of newt, and toe of frog,
> Wool of bat, and tongue of dog,
> Adder's fork, and blind-worm's sting,
> Lizard's leg, and howlet's wing,
> For a charm of powerful trouble,
> Like a hell-broth boil and bubble.

From the recipe of the second *Weird Sister* from Shakespeare's *Macbeth*.

### Familiars

The black cat has become the 'familiar' (companion) of witches to help them with their spells. Blackbirds and crows, among other lower animals were other creatures to which the witch has been traditionally attached. Cold blooded animals like toads and frogs were also regarded as suitable pets for witches. The fish was never mentioned, possibly due to the fact that the fish is an ancient Christian symbol as well as an emblem of chastity. A witch may have one imp or several. One witch confessed that the Devil gave her two little dogs and a mole. Another witch said she had four familiars.

The association between witches and the animal kingdom is far more complex and its roots go far back to the beginning of sorcery. Animal skins and masks were used in witchcraft fertility rites. It was believed that witches could turn themselves, at will, into a wolf or a cat.

As late as the 19th century, cases are recorded, in Russia, that peasant women were ordered by their masters to nurse bear cubs that were being reared for sport. The suckling of the familiar by the witch reveals the true nature of the relationship between them and on the evil interdependence.

101

Witch with her Familiar

A 16th century Somerset witch stated that "her familiar doth commonly suck her right breast about seven at night, in the shape of a little cat of dunnish colour . . . and when she is suckt, she is in a kind of 'trance.'

## The Salem Witch Hunt

Hundreds of years ago, most American colonists firmly believed in Satan and his demons. Many of the people of New England were terrified of these demons. The sermons of the early Puritan preachers were often filled with fiery warnings to avoid the tricks of the Devil and his servants such as witches, warlocks and imps.

While many of the stories about witches were true, there were instances where the accusations were false. One woman named Dinah Sylvester accused the wife of William Holmes, one of Miles Standish's lieutenants, of being a witch. Dinah swore in court that the woman had changed herself into a bear and attacked her. However, the judge did not believe Dinah's story and ruled against her. He fined her five pounds and ordered her to be whipped for telling such a tale.

It was only a matter of time until in Boston, in 1648, an accused witch was found guilty but not executed. Two years later, however, a witch was hanged in the Connecticut colony. By 1692 in Salem, Massachusetts, twenty people were reported to have been found guilty and executed.

## Isabel Gowdie

The name of Isabel Gowdie continually is heard in connection with British witchcraft. Isabel Gowdie was an attractive, red-haired girl, married to a farmer living on the edge of Lochloy near Auldearne. She seems to have married young, and quickly grew bored on the lonely farm. Childless, and married to a boorish husband, Isabel due to her discontentment is said to have become the victim of Satan.

According to Isabel, in 1647, a 'man in grey' accosted her on the downs and she became a willing follower of him. He baptized her that same evening in Auldearne kirk, giving her the name of 'Janet', a typical non-Christian name. Becoming a dedicated follower of the 'man in grey', Isabel is said to have been given the witch's mark upon her by this man, who then proceeded to suck her blood.

The 'man in grey' was later found to be the Devil-god of a local coven. Isabel was eventually given the names of the thirteen others in the 'coven' and the names of the personal spirits or fairies who attended each member:

> Ilk one of us has a Spirit to wait upon us, when we please to call upon him. I remember not all the Spirits' names; but there is one called Swein, which waits upon the said Margaret Wilson, in Auldearne; he is still (always) clothed in grass-green; and the said Margaret Wilson has a nickname called Pikle nearest the Wind. The next Spirit is called Rorie, who waits upon Bessie Wilson, in Auldearne; he is still clothed in yellow; and her nickname is Throw the Corn Yard . . . Jean Marten is Maid to the Coven that I am of; and her nickname is Over the Dyke with It, because the Devil always takes the Maiden in his hand next to him, when we dance Gillatrypes; and when we would leap . . . he and she will say "Over the Dyke with it!"

Isabel tells that her spirit is called the Read Riever and habitually wore black. She believed those beings to be supernaturals, but in reality, the 'spirits' were male members of the organization dressed up like the Devil. The dances suggest the traditional rituals, such as follow-my-leader, and

A Celebration of Witches

the circles 'widdershins', against the course of the sun. The meetings, which were held regularly, ended with a phallic orgy.

Isabel relates that she and her friends copulated with their spirits and also with the Devil himself. The Devil's person suggested some sort of artificial phallus of horn or leather. "His members are exceeding great and long and he is a rough man, cold as ice."

Eating, drinking, and making mischief usually were included on these occasions. Isabel claimed that she and other witches had the power to turn themselves into hares or cats. She had a little horse on which she rode to meetings, crying to it, "Horse and Hattock in the Devil's name!"

## English Witchcraft

A traveler through the eastern countries of England, particularly East Anglia, will notice certain monuments dedicated to the victims of religious persecutions during the reign of Mary I in the first half of the 16th century, in which no less than 277 Protestants were burned by the Romanists. After Elizabeth I had succeeded to the throne, there exploded a violent hatred for all things that were 'popish' and a demand for radical reform. It was during this time that reformers sought the elimination of the practice of the magic and sorcery that had been permitted to function almost unchecked by the Church of Rome. Essex, the center of dissent, became the leader of this reformation and demanded a clearing out of every kind of sorcery.

During the reign of Edward VI the *Witchcraft Act* of 1542, the first legislation against witchcraft, was repealed. An attempt to reinstitute this law was made during the reign of Mary. Then in 1560 laws were finally passed that prohibited sorcery. Bishop Jewel delivered a sermon before Elizabeth in 1560 in which he stressed the need for legal action against magicians, or witches. He went on to demand that the laws touching such malefactors be put in due execution. In 1563 the Convocation of the Church of England urged stronger penalties upon the practitioners of witchcraft, and in that same year the *Elizabethan Witchcraft Act* was passed into law. This law imposed the penalty of death for murder by sorcery, and the pillory and imprisonment for witchcraft of a less lethal character.

The first person known to have been executed in England after the new Act had come into existence was 63-year-old Agnes Waterhouse of Hatfield Peverel in Essex, who was hanged at Chelmsford in 1566 for the crime of bewitching William Fynee to death. Her familiar, a cat named Sathan, was believed to be supporting evidence of her guilt.

## German Witchcraft
In Germany, notorious for its witch persecutions, the law ordered that suspected witches should be tortured into confessing. Some of the terrible torture inflicted on these 16th century witches and witch suspects included disembowelling, beheading, gouging out the eyes, cutting off the ear or hand, and flogging.

In areas where the trials had been in process for some time, gangs of children 'hounded' suspected witches with unusual venom, before the victims were imprisoned. Without understanding the seriousness of the matter, the children in play would accuse each other of sorcery and boast that they could bewitch people. They would invent stories so convincingly that the authorities would follow the 'lead' with a vengence. The outcome sometimes brought the small children to trials not only as witnesses but also as defendants.

## French Witchcraft
Witchcraft in Europe combined two different ingredients.

One was using spells and potions to work black magic or white magic. The second was the belief that witches were the armed warriors of the Devil. This witchcraft was entirely dedicated to evil and purposely sought the help of Satan in order to carry out its wishes. The witch was now faced with severe accusations which led to torturing them until they confessed.

For the 'new witch' religion the Sabbath was the meeting at which the Devil was worshipped. The earliest account of it which has come down through the centuries is that of a woman named Anne-Marie de Georgel, who confessed that many years before a tall dark man, who had fiery eyes and was clothed in skins, appeared to her while she was washing. He is said to have asked her to give herself to him. When she agreed, he breathed in her ear and on the following Saturday, merely by willing it, she was taken to the witches' meeting. The meeting was presided over by a 'goat', which taught her secret ways to work evil. It is recorded that from that time on Anna-Marie de Georgel continued down the path of the destruction of others.

## Basque Witchcraft

Witches and wizards were intensely active in the Basque from the later part of the 15th century to the early years of the 17th century; so much so that their reputation spread throughout Europe.

The Basques are a people of unknown origin, living along the coasts of northern Spain and southern France. From as early as the 3rd century BC they were famous for their skill in predicting the future from the flight of birds.

Many Basque witches confessed to have made ointments with toads' blood and babies' hearts and to having trafficked with the Devil, in the form of a man who had a horn in his forehead and long teeth protruding from his mouth.

## Italian Witchcraft

In the early 17th century, three friars were convicted of casting spells and holding a mortuary mass in an attempt to shorten the life of Pope Urban VIII.

Two strands must be distinguished in Italian witchcraft. The women dealing in love and healing potions, and those who told fortunes. In country regions the 'pastoral' witch was left unharmed until the outburst against witchcraft provoked by the Inquisition at the beginning of the 15th century.

The Catholic church's attitude toward sorcery, it has been written, was a passion for knowledge and a desire to see into the future, using part-magical, part-scientific processes. Popes, kings and learned men studied astrology and thereby indulged in the same practices as that of the sorcerers. Anyone seeking to probe the unknown was believed to be disobeying God's laws, moving toward heresy or in partnership with the Devil.

Throughout history Italian witches, in particular, seemed to have been making use of *poisons*. With their potions the witches were apparently following the national tradition. One of the earliest examples of secular legislation against such practices was instigated by the 12th century Norman king of the Two Sicilies, Roger II. He stated that the concoction of love potions, whether they worked or not, was a crime. In 1181 the Doge Orlo Malipieri of Venice also passed laws punishing poisoning and sorcery.

## Swedish Witchcraft

Although the Scandinavian countries conducted few organized witch hunts, the fear of witches existed and could arouse hysteria and panic. One such case was the witches of Mora in Sweden where witches were accused of taking children to a mysterious place called the Blocula where they were believed to be enrolled in the service of the Devil.

The Lutheran pastor of Elfdale in central Sweden reported to his bishop that a girl named Gertrude Svensen had learned the art of magical incantation from a servant, Marit Honsdotter, and had stolen several children of the district for 'the evil genius', the Devil.

## Beelzebub

Under questioning as to being a witch, a Monk of the Abbey of Stablo in Netherlands confessed in 1595 that the demonic being worshipped by witches at their Sabbaths was Beelzebub. They kissed his footprints and before their feast said grace in the name of Beelzebub. Two Frenchmen of the early 17th century also reported that witches blessed their food in Beelzebub's name and called him the 'creator and preserver of all things'; in other words they regarded him as their god.

## Belial

The 'demon of lies', Belial means 'without worth.' Depraved debauchees are sometimes called 'sons of Belial' in the Old Testament, but in the *Testaments of the Twelve Patriarchs* of the late centuries BC Belial achieves much higher rank as chief of devils, prince of deceit, the malicious one, the tempter, the ruler of evil inclinations and the master of hypocrites. In one of the Dead Sea Scrolls, *The War of the Sons of Light and the Sons of Darkness,* he is the leader of the forces of evil. 'But for corruption thou hast made Belial, an angel of hostility. All his dominion is in darkness, and his purpose is to bring about wickedness and guilt.'

II Cornithians 6:14 says: *Be ye not unequally yoked together with unbelievers: for what fellowship hath righteousness with unrighteousness? and what communion hath light with darkness?*

## The Witchhunt

Men in tribal societies, through beliefs in witchcraft, tried to explain the otherwise inexplicable occurrence of their particular misfortunes, and second, they held their personal enemies responsible. These men tried to explain why it was that at a certain time and certain place, a certain person, whose life had been relatively normal up to this time, suffered a particular misfortune — such as disease, the death of a family member, or animals, the blighting of crops, accidents, and so on. His 'bad luck' was ascribed to the malevolence of an enemy, who brought this upon him by supernatural or occult powers.

In many tribal societies witches were considered most likely to be a relative of the actual victim, or the person who was the guardian of the victim. One village might reject a divination quite acceptable to another and go to a diviner of his own choice, or a divination acceptable at one time might be rejected at another time.

A witch usually was the medium to bring misfortune to a certain person. However, in European hunts for witches, the whole community, including the church, would get very involved. Since witchcraft was closely identified with heresy, and an abomination in God's eyes, the church believed that it was its duty to root out these heretics and witches.

**To be ignorant of Satan's devices is death!**

# 7

# BLACK MASS AND BLACK MAGIC

### The Black Mass

Little is known of the early history of the Black Mass. The rites and ceremonies of the Christian church have been recorded from its early childhood until now, but there does not exist one single document describing the rites of the Black Mass at its inception. These rites are, to a large degree, magical, and are unlike Christianity or any other theology.

Satanism can be divided roughly into two branches: the *Luciferians* and the *Palladists.* The first mentioned believe that evil is good; and that the Devil (or dark forces) can offer abundant material life, together with the obtaining of all material desires, by yielding to every temptation without thought of morality, self-sacrifice or duty to others. The Palladists, however, openly worship the Devil as such, taking their stand by the goat Deity (Baphomet of the Templars) and wallowing in evil for its own sake.

During the *Black Mass,* a small group of people sit in front of a table covered with a purple velvet altar cloth, lit with candles. Over the altar hangs an upside down cross and a picture of the Devil, half-human, half-beast. A high priest, dressed in bishop's robes and wearing an inverted cross, stands by the table. He throws a larger cross to the floor. *"Shemhaforash!"* he shouts. (This is probably the most powerful word uttered in Satanic worship. As was written earlier in this book, according to the Talmud, this secret mystical word was spoken by God when He created the world.) The Satanic priest then spits upon the cross, and with an obscene gesture cries, *"Hail Satan!"* The Devil worshippers then repeat *The Lord's Prayer* backwards as well as make mockery of the ordinances of the church.[1]

Initiation of a Witch

*Nudity is prevalent in the worship of Satan. During the initiation ceremony of a witch the initiate lies naked on the altar, is symbolically 'sacrificed' to the sun god. A mysterious force within her own body is believed to heighten the power within the witch. That power is believed to be obstructed when clothing is worn. The delusion of the Satanists is that they will gain pleasure and enjoyment in this world, especially of a sensual nature; and that in a coming age, Satan will overcome the God of the Christians and return to the heaven from which he was once banished. The followers will then share the fruits of eternal power with Satan's spirit forces.*[2]

The *Black Mass* is the most blasphemous ceremony in the whole performance of black magic. While festivals of evil and witches' Sabbaths were held long before Christianity came into existence, the mass, being essentially a perversion of the highest and holiest ceremony of the Catholic church, was introduced as the predominant feature of the Sabbaths and the supreme ceremony of evil performed by sorcerers and workers of the *'Left-Hand Path.'*

Rollo Ahmed, an Egyptian by birth, acquired his knowledge of the 'secret art' from his father's family. However, his mother was a native of the West Indies and while Rollo was still in his teens the family moved from Egypt, living in the 'devil-ridden islands' and the forests of the Yucatan, Guiana and Brazil. There he learned, firsthand, about the primitive magic of the forest Indians and also Voodoo and the use of 'obeahs.' Later he explored Europe and Asia for further knowledge of the mysteries and for a while lived in Burma, where he became a practitioner of Raja Yoga.

Among other books, such as *A Black Art,* Rollo Ahmed wrote *The Complete Book of Witchcraft* in which he writes: ". . . this work is chiefly concerned with man's evil perversion of the Sacrament in the ceremony of the Black Mass, the chief feature of which was originally human sacrifice — flesh and blood. The performance of the Black Mass could only be accompanied by a renegade priest, one who had taken the vows of the Holy Mother Church, but had either been unfrocked or had turned his back upon her. When witchcraft was at its height in the Middle Ages, the ceremony of the Black Mass was celebrated almost openly and the priests and clergy had to guard their churches closely against sacrilege. As it was, the graveyards were frequently the scene of witches' Sabbaths, and the church of North Berwick on the borders of England and Scotland was notorious for the celebration of the 'Sacrament of Hell.' In the ceremony, the officiating priest was usually accompanied by female assistants, clad in a travesty of the garments of the Church, and the Host itself was made in the form of small black wafers, mixed with revolting substances and stamped with obscene images or the impress (head) of Satan. Sometimes, however, the wafers were of a dark red colour, resembling dried blood. The Chalice used was occasionally of wood and metal, but frequently the hollowed skull of a criminal served this purpose. The fluid within the Chalice was blood mixed with vile substances; or in another variation of the ceremony the urine of the participants, especially that of women, would be substituted.

"There were many slight differences in the form of procedure, and even in the appurtenances employed, but the main features of the blasphemous ceremony remained the same. In some cases the altar was covered with a black linen cloth; in others it was left bare, or was merely a rough slab of stone on which were placed the candles, bowls or skulls to be used. The candles were composed of human fat mixed with sulphur and other substances, and were always black. The candlesticks represented the heavenly bodies — sun, moon and stars — and were made of ebony. The 'incense' used was a mixture of asafoetida, sulphur and alum, or other herbs of obnoxious odour. The priest's vestments were sometimes black, with a white silk cape embroidered with fir cones, while on other occasions he and his assistants wore violet or scarlet robes."[3]

Ahmed reports that Henri de Valois, son of Catherine de' Medici practiced the black art in one of the turrets of his castle in the Bois de Vincennes. Upon his death a most interesting discovery was made: a cross, and two silver figures of satyrs turning their backs upon the cross and carrying behind them large crystal bowls that were evidently used for drugs or libations. Among the relics the dressed skin of a child was also found.

At the time of the death of King Charles IX of France, Catherine de' Medici decided to consult the oracle of the *Bleeding Head.* The offspring of an infamous family, known for its cruelty, Catherine instigated the massacre of St. Bartholomew. Maintaining the services of an apostate priest, who was adept in the black art and accustomed to working sorcery, Catherine ordered the torture of people through *wax simulacra.*

For the oracle of the 'Bleeding Head' a child was required, who was good-looking, pure and sweet-natured. The vicious procedure went like this:

A boy was chosen and prepared in secret for his first communion by the palace chaplain. Then, at midnight on an appointed day, the Black Mass was celebrated by Catherine's sorcerer in the chamber of the dying King, the Queen-Mother also being present. In the room an altar had been erected, with the figure of the Devil above it and under his feet a reversed cross. After consecrating two wafers, one black and one white, the child victim was brought in, dressed as for baptism, and given the white wafer. Immediately after having received his first communion, the little victim's head was struck off with one blow from a sword upon the very steps of the altar. The head was placed, bleeding and quivering, upon the black wafer, and then transferred to a table upon which lights were burning. The priest next pronounced an incantation, and the demon was commanded to speak through the head of the poor child, in reply to a secret question of the King's that could not be spoken aloud. It was recorded that a strange voice did, in fact, speak; but what it said is unknown and the sorcery failed in its main object — the King died.

Primitive people in many parts of the world practice a similar form of black magic with the heads of newborn infants placed in a bowl of blood.

While most of the sacrificial victims of the Black Mass were women, young children and even babies were not exempt, and on occasion, men were sacrificed as well. All were slain with ingenious torture and cruelty, their bowels and entrails being literally torn out, while, when women were the victims, their reproductive organs were chosen as the point of torture. Little children were treated in the same way; the Devil, or at least his followers, evidently took unholy pleasure in the sacrifice of the young.

The Black Mass was always performed between eleven o'clock and midnight, but the subsequent revellings lasted until dawn. To add to the perversion of the Holy Sacrament, which many believe should be taken while fasting, participants consumed huge quantities of food and wine before and after the main part of Satan's banquet. While it is not known for sure, some early accounts place the time of the sacrifice of the victim before the actual celebration of the Black Mass as the culmination point of the hideous ritual.

A mock confession followed *The Lord's Prayer,* then the celebrant made an inverse sign of the Cross with his left hand. The Chalice would then be passed around, to be filled with the urine of the participants or dipped in the blood of the sacrifice. Next came the elevation of the Host, which was received with wild screams and hideous yells from the congregation. The priest then stabbed the Host with the same knife which he had used for killing the victim, and the wafers composing it were dipped into the blood. After that,

Satanic Symbol

the Host was thrown upon the ground, where the priest spat upon it and all the participants rushed forward with growls and screams to trample it underfoot. The final desecration was the out-pouring of the contents of the Chalice upon the crushed remains.

It was commonly believed that if anyone had an enemy, and at a celebration of the Black Mass secured a portion of

117

the blood-stained Host and holding it up called out the name of the person with curses, he or she would surely die or be injured. Since nearly everyone had an enemy, or at least someone to whom they wished harm, participants, feverishly scrambled for the trampled Host.

The Black Mass ceremony ended in feasting (often upon the remains of the sacrificial victim) with every imaginable exhibition of gluttony, after which all possible forms of sexual license were indulged in by those who were not too overcome by excessive eating and drinking.

While there were many variations in the performance of the Mass, not all were performed with the same kind of debauchery. In some instances the 'celebration' was held by a few persons or by the members of some secret society. Often the Black Mass was performed with the express purpose of cursing some person or bringing disaster and downfall to individuals and systems.

The main feature of the witches' Sabbaths was the Black Mass, and if the witches did not actually attend them in any magical manner they certainly participated in the abominations of *Satan's Sacrament*. This later replaced earlier pagan rites connected with Isis, Diana or Astarte — all different aspects of a single conception of the female deity. Those taking part in these orgies abandoned clothes entirely or donned strange cloaks resembling the wings of bats and wore hideous masks representing birds, animals and reptiles. In later times, however, on all such occasions all possible coverings were stripped off, and naked men and women, joining hands, danced in a ring around the altar with their backs turned to it. At the Sabbaths the Devil was either impersonated by his priest or an evil materialization, who received neophytes and children, and presented his posterior for a kiss of his followers, with unprintable additions. During the performances of the sexual orgies that followed, there are many accounts that the Devil had intercourse with people of both sexes.

It is understandable how the sexual involvement became interwoven with the Black Mass and the witches' Sabbaths; quite apart from the obvious reason of giving fullest expression to man's lowest passions.

Says Ahmed, *"The inaugurators of the Black Mass and witches' Sabbaths were undoubtedly steeped in Left-Hand occultism, or the black art, and knew how the great generative power might be abused and perverted both on the psychic and material planes. By inciting lust, and devising every imaginable means for its expression, they turned the great force and power of creation towards the energizing of foul shapes, disease and destruction in every possible form.* The ordinary participants, inflamed with drug and drink, maddened with blood and sadistic excitement, would certainly have had no thought but of expressing their lowest and filthiest impulses, and of wallowing in a mad phantasmagoria of sexual lust. On the other hand, the officiating priest, or sorcerers, undoubtedly used the degraded release of man's highest potency with deliberate intent."[4]

— — — —

In the sixteenth and seventeenth centuries Satanism was 'not' a *popular parlour game*. Persons thought to be witches were regarded as extremely dangerous and no punishment could be too severe. "Confession was regarded as an essential element in the course of bringing a witch to justice and to this end torture was freely applied"[5] says Frank Smythe, in his book, *Modern Witchcraft*.

Wilhelm Pressel gives us a full account of the first day's torture of a woman accused of witchcraft in Prossneck in 1629:

"The proceedings start early in the morning. The woman's hands are bound, the hangman cuts her hair and throws alcohol over her head, setting it on fire to burn it to its roots. He then places strips of sulphur in her armpits and burns them. She is hauled up to the ceiling and left hanging there for three hours while he enjoys a leisurely breakfast. Thus refreshed he throws alcohol over her back and burns it, suspends her from the ceiling with heavy weights on her feet, forces her body down on a plank stuck with nails, squeezes her thumbs and big toes in a vice, and hangs her from the ceiling again. During this period she faints several times."[6]

He then squeezes her legs in a vice and follows this with flogging with a rawhide whip. He puts her thumbs and big toes back into the vice and goes out to lunch for three hours. The afternoon consists largely of whipping.

After such a beating anyone is likely to confess to almost anything. Mr. Pressel continues:

"Her feet were crushed and her body stretched out to greater length, she screamed piteously and said all was true that they had demanded of her: she drank the blood of children whom she stole on her night flights and she had murdered about sixty infants. She named twenty other women who had been with her at the Sabbats, and said the wife of a late burgomaster presided over the fights and banquets."[7]

One Burgomaster of Bamberg accused of witchcraft in 1628, Johannes Junius, wrote to his daughter:

"When at last the executioner led me back into the cell he said to me, 'Sir, I beg you, for God's sake, confess something whether it be true or not. Invent something, for you cannot endure the torture which you will be put to: and even if you bear it all, yet you will not escape, not even if you were an earl, but one torture will follow another until you say you are a witch.'"[8]

Lest the above-quoted author's explicit description of the terrible torture put upon witch 'suspects' cause you to become *sympathetic* toward witches, bear in mind the author's obvious *liberal* position concerning witchcraft and *God's commandment toward those who practice it . . . death.* Exodus 22:18 says *Thou shalt not suffer a witch to live.*

120

— — — —

"The sorcerer of the seventeenth and eighteenth centuries constantly performed the Black Mass for reasons of political intrigue, especially in France. On the night of the murder of Louis XVI in 1793, a large number of these people and their followers assembled to celebrate the *Eucharist of Hell*. Towards the end of the eighteenth century there sprang up a society at Linburg, calling themselves *The Goats*. They met at night in a secret chapel to perform the Black Mass, after which they put on masks of goats with long gowns and set out in bands to commit rape and murder, plundering and robbing everyone who was unlucky enough to cross their path. The tribunal of Foquemont over a period condemned four hundred of this society to be hanged, but the Goats were not stamped out until 1780."[9]

## Voodoo

*Voodoo, the origins of which lay in darkest Africa, is one of the vilest, cruellest and most debased forms of worship ever devised by man. It blends African religions, Roman Catholicism and Indian mysticism. Voodoo was linked to Roman Catholicism for years because of the necessity to disguise the 'banned' ceremonies.*

Voodooists believe in a 'consciousness' that can be manipulated for good or evil. Some of their gods are *Legba*, roughly a counterfeit Jesus Christ, *Obacala*, the god of water, and *Erzulie*, goddess of love. A priest is called a *houngan* and a priestess is a *mambo*. Much sexual perverseness and corruption permeates all aspects of the voodoo religion.

As of March, 1987, the people of Haiti can openly practice voodoo, which had been outlawed for fifty years. At ceremonies staged for tourists, participants might bite off the head of a chicken or walk on burning coals. Some of the cultural aspects of voodoo include herbal medicine, ritual dances, and the color and style of the clothing. As one person observed, voodoo is not only a religion, but it also infiltrates all aspects of life in Haiti.

## Black Magic

In early times, and among more modern primitive races, phallic worship had little or nothing to do with sorcery. During those times the sex forces were regarded as protective and beneficial and were invoked to operate against evil. They symbolized life as opposed to death, and fertility and plenty as against barrenness, disease and destruction.

It was believed that the phallus had power to subdue the attacks of demons and the *Evil Eye;* and that the female organs were potent over elemental disturbances, thus a woman who exposed her body could calm a storm. Man's virility was typified by the snake, and worshipped and accepted as the symbol of wisdom, and solar deities were reverenced with phallic rites. Celebrations were held heralding the Spring of the year and the sowing of crops were accompanied by rites of sexual intercourse to stimulate fertility, and in Autumn festivals of harvest were welcomed in the same manner with happiness and thanksgiving.

Nearly all *amulets* originally appeared in phallic formations, but in time this was replaced with 'hands' representing the male and female reproductive organs; the male organ being the shape of part of an arm with the fist clenched and the female organ a hand alone and open. Most people are familiar with such little ornaments made in coral. The triangle, pyramid, or cone is but a form of the phallus reduced to simple lines; and most Egyptian amulets were of this origin, with the possible exception of the Scarab (a symbol of resurrection) and the *Eye of Horns.*

PHALLICISM WAS, THEREFORE, AT THE ROOT OF

MOST RELIGIONS, and was definitely believed to be the opponent of evil and darkness. However, as time went on and magic became identified with so many of the religious customs and ceremonies, the phallic aspect became an outlet for men's passions.

Religious sodomy was practiced by male prostitutes in the Hebrew temple groves, which was one of the abominations of Israel that Josiah cleared away. II Kings 23 tells us that Josiah broke down their houses which were near the temple, and drove the Sodomites out, burning their groves and scattering the ashes on the graves of the people. At the same time he 'put away' all the wizards and workers with familiar spirits, destroyed the idols and images, filling up the site of the groves with the bodies of the dead.

Witchcraft and sorcery, being in themselves evil, naturally seized upon the sexual instinct and passions to pervert them to their own ends. In Europe the witches observed Sabbaths by shedding their clothing and engaging in every conceivable lustful impulse, this condition being further induced by the Ungent which they smeared on their bodies.

From the end of the fifteenth century there was an increase in the casting of spells and enchantments and indulging in performances of the Black Mass. There grew an insatiable interest in lewd indulgences and a taking part in rituals which entailed entire nakedness or partial exposure. Many of the so-called rites of these secret societies were only an excuse for men and women to indulge in sexplay and lustful gratification, frequently of an abnormal kind.

LOVE POTIONS CONTAINED VARIOUS ODIOUS SUBSTANCES MIXED WITH CERTAIN HUMAN FLUIDS, ACCORDING TO THE SEX OF THE WOULD-BE LOVER, WHILE SPECIAL CHARMS WERE MADE AFTER THE FASHION OF THE GENITAL ORGANS. TODAY, THESE PHALLIC TALISMANS CAN BE SEEN

EVERWHERE AND ARE WORN WITHOUT ANY CONCEALMENT.

In Scotland, where the rites of *Hallow's E'en* are still observed, the original significance of many of the customs has long been forgotten, games with apples and candles figure very largely; but apples are a fruit with a phallic symbolism.

In spite of the fact that *candles* had memorially represented the phallus upon altars, a fact unknown to the population at large, many architectural designs upon buildings have the same origin.

In medieval times sex rites were used in necromancy and for invoking the presence of demons or elementals. The virile life forces of the body were believed to be more potent than the blood, and both were used to invoke demons. These methods entailed the exercise of sex perversion. In Europe, Asia and Africa, when necromancy was performed with the dead bodies of women, someone would have intercourse with the corpse as a preliminary means of revitalizing it.

The sacrifice of their virginity to Satan was expected of the women who took part in the rites of black magic. The sex act was performed first with the chief officiator, who was sometimes disguised as the Devil, and then with other participants.

It has been believed, among all nations and races, that blood possesses the vital essence of life and an incalculable mystic potency. The precious blood was poured out freely so that it would cause the living to have courage, vitality and strength. Blood was never to be 'spilled.' For this reason, many medieval tortures did not incorporate the shedding of blood, lest those who inflicted the torture be held guilty of the blood of their victims.

Beastiality was commonplace among the sorcerers of the

Australian Aborgines, usually at the time when the magician was supposed to turn into an animal. This custom was familiar to the early Egyptians and Assyrians. In some of the cults of Isis, and the forbidden idolatries of Israel, both priest and priestess performed the lewd ritual with sacrificial animals immediately before their slaughter.

When sorcery was sought as a revenge for a gilted lover, figures were made of wood, wax, clay or dough, according to nationality, with huge, disproportionate reproductive organs, which were subjected to various tortures. This was done in order to inflict suffering upon the unfaithful lover.

## Jewish Magic

It is believed that during their captivity in Egypt the Jews learned about magic. The first reference to magic appears in the Pentateuch.

Like the other sorcerers, Hebrews believed that the best gift to give evil spirits was blood. The attitude toward magic was that its accomplishments were only temporary, and that they could be undone by other magicians. Due, in part, to the fact that it involved nakedness and gross sexual practices, witchcraft and sorcery were looked upon with deep aversion as being impure and lewd and those who practiced it were depraved. Witches were classed with harlots, and their practices an abomination.

Hebrews, except for the orthodox Jew, generally vascillated between orthodox religion and paganism and magic. The orthodox Jew saw magic of any kind as abhorrent, and the word magic stood for one who dealt with dark and evil forces.

## Discerning of Spirits

Young boys were used for the discerning of spirits. A male child, seven years of age, who had been chosen for the ceremony, has his hand anointed with olive oil and into it is placed a crystal. The magician then seats himself on a three-legged stool, drawing the child between his thighs with his back turned — so that the man's mouth can be close to the child's ear — and the magician can take the child's hand. Then, facing the sun, the magician repeats in the child's ear: *"Aungil, I adjure thee in the name of the lord god, god of truth, god-keeper of the hosts, Alpga, Aidu, that thou shalt send on from thee three angels."*[10] The boy is now supposed to see a figure like that of a man, and the charm is repeated two more times. After that, when the three figures appear, the boy says to them, *"Your coming be in peace."* and proceeds to ask the required questions. If there is not an answer, the child is to address the figure as follows: *"KASPAR, KELEI, EMAR, the master and I adjure thee with a second adjunction, that thou wilt tell me that thing"*[11] — whatever the required knowledge might be.

**Does the name KASPAR (Casper) remind you of anything you've seen and heard on television?**

All the usual paraphernalia of magic-wands, candles, black-handled knives, circles, pentagrams, and more were used by the Hebrew magician. Medieval sorcerers and necromancers were indebted to the *Cabala* for most of their evocations. The former also used bowls inscribed with the names of night spirits. These may have been used as crystals; the *Talmud* refers to "the Princes and rulers of all shining objects and crystals," which appears to indicate the spirits who manifested by such means.

Manasseh was one who observed times and enchantments, practiced witchcraft and dealt with familiar spirits and wizards. Balaam was numbered among them, and taught the daughters of Moab to be witches. The *witch of Endor* was the prime example of Jewish necromancy.

*Kischuph,* was a form of sorcery that was practiced

extensively. By this means witches and magicians changed themselves into animals, and were able to cover great distances in a short space of time. Disease and death was the result of the attacks from these animals. Women who were involved in this form of sorcery had made a covenant unto the *Schedim,* and met them at certain times to dance with them, and visited the spirits that appear to them in the shape of goats. When their activities became known, many women were killed by stoning.

Jewish necromancers, male and female worked with familiar spirits, called *Ob*. The witch of Endor, conjured her own particular 'familiar' with ceremonies and enchantments. On one occasion, she asked Saul whom he wished to have raised from the dead. (It was also a custom of Hebrew necromancers to use mummified bodies for purposes of divination. This was another practice learned from Egyptians sorcerers. Heads were consulted, too — first-born children were slain, their heads cut off and salted and embalmed. Gold plates were prepared with invocations engraved around the edges, and the heads mounted upon them. The heads were kept very carefully, and consulted on special occasions.)

Simon Magus was a Jewish sorcerer who bewitched the people of Samaria into thinking he possessed divine attributes. Simon Magus seems to have had a thirst for power over others, and was believed to have asked to join Jesus' disciples. Rejected by the disciples, Simon Magus began to imitate their works and miracles and even permitted himself to be worshipped. He declared that he was a manifestation of God, and claimed a divine origin for his Greek medium, Helen. He imitated Christianity in the reverse sense, affirming the eternal reign of evil. Traveling to Rome, he was called before Nero, who eventually made him a court magician.

– – – –

Many of the 'rain-making' ceremonies are of a sexual nature. In many parts of Africa drought is thought to be due to the result of a woman who concealed the fact that she had a miscarriage. The witch doctor gathers all the females of his district and makes them confess. A black ox is placed in a container with four openings, North, South, East and West. While chanting, little girls pour water into the container, which escapes through the channels to the four points of the compass. Next, women strip naked and dance a rain dance. After the dance they begin to dig up the remains of the abortions and miscarriages, water or urine being emptied into the graves. When nighttime arrives the remnants are reinterred and rain is expected.

Among tribes where the customs regarding sexual intercourse are liberal, the rain dance and burials are followed by gross sexual license; at night the men go to the huts of various women and wife-swapping is the norm.

In certain parts of Europe, where black magic societies exist, circumcision is performed on male members, the flesh being consumed as a sacrifice by the members of the organization. In some parts of Asia the whole or parts of the genital organs are amputated as a sacrificial offering. The ceremonial shaving of the pubic hair of both sexes is common among sorcerers throughout the world. Once the hair is shaven, it is either sprinkled with blood and buried or burnt with other substances.

While man continues in his tireless effort to satisfy the flesh, his *spirit* goes unsatisfied. Peace is found only in Jesus Christ.

**Black Mass and Black Magic equals death!**

# 8

# MODERN-DAY WITCHCRAFT

**Witches For Halloween?**

The modern sophisticate, who does not realistically face the evil and danger surrounding this time of year, may say, "Witches are for Halloween. It is a time for children to visit the neighborhood to get candy and apples. There is no harm in celebrating Halloween with its witches and devils." To some, 'witches' are a figment of the imaginations of the superstitious seventeenth century Salem primitives.

If witches are for Halloween — a thing of the past, then why are so many young people and older ones alike being swept into the grips of Satan by 'dabbling' in those things which relate to him?

The pagan belief is that out of the union of the god and goddess came the universe, and between them they control the seasons, bringing fertility to crops and animals, and bestow magical powers upon their followers. To refresh your memory, the seasons are: the Spring equinox, on March 21; May Eve or Beltane, on April 30; the Summer solstice, mid-summer on June 22; August Eve, or Lammastide, on August 1; the Autumn equinox on September 21; Halloween on October 31; the Winter solstice, or Yule, on December 21; and Candlemas on February 2. Sabbat is the name given to the meetings held by the witches on these days. Another Sabbat is held on nights when the moon is full, in honor of the goddess. Many 'covens' 'draw down' the goddess, symbolized by the moon, into a priestess in a trance, who then 'incarnates' the goddess. Nobody knows just how many Wiccans and other Neo-Pagans there are in the United States, but there are more than enough for Beltane and the seven other seasonal Sabbats to be celebrated around the country.

Leading universities are now reporting capacity enrollment in courses on witchcraft. Book sales on the occult and Satanism have soared and high schools across this country have their campus 'witches and warlocks.'

Occult experimentation from astrology and the Ouija board to slumber party seances have led many unsuspecting youth down the road to emotional and spiritual slavery through participation in Satan worship.

## Modern Satanism

"Satanism advocates practicing a modified form of the Golden Rule"[1] says Anton Szandor La Vey, founder of the *Church of Satan* in San Francisco, in the *Satanic Bible*. *"Our interpretation of this rule is 'Do unto others as they do unto you.'"*[2]

This comment by Anton La Vey clearly illustrates the principle on which Satanism is based. Things which are backward, upside down, the wrong way round are symbolically connected with the Devil as the power which seeks to overturn the order and worship of God, and the essence of Satanism is the reversal of Christian and conventional values. To the Satanist the Christian God is evil and the Devil is good. The *Prince of Darkness* is believed to be the true Lord of Light.

Other quotes from the Satanic Bible are, *"Blessed are the strong for they shall possess the earth."*[3] and *"If a man smite you on one cheek, smash him on the other!"*[4]

Christian principles and moral values are rejected and

ridiculed by the Satanist. Instead of love and mercy, the Satanist devotes himself to dominance, cruelty, lust and all fierce and passionate emotions.

To the Satanist, two of the most hated virtues possessed by Christians are *humility* and *purity*. This is not surprising. After all, wasn't pride the cause of Satan's expulsion from heaven?

To the Christian, to delight in all pleasures of the senses is sinful and unclean. He opposes this worldliness and the ruthless struggle for power and pleasure on earth, and in and through the flesh.

Modern Satanism has received much of its impetus from 19th century literature, from its rebellion against Victorian values, especially in relation to sex, and from its fierce hatred against Christianity.


## Aleister Crowley

Aleister Crowley (1875-1947) was an *eccentric,* a writer of books on magic who strove to assume the *mantle of magician.* Born of a father who preached the doctrines of the Plymouth Brethren, Crowley resisted faith in Christ and turned to Satan. Crowley took a fancy to the *False Prophet,* to the *Beast, whose number was 666,* and to the *Scarlet Woman* characters.

In 1896, Crowley met a man named Mathers and became involved with a magical society known as the *Hermetic Order of the Golden Dawn,* accepting all the vows and obligations, he took the magical title of *Perdurabo* (I will endure to the end).

Crowley moved to a flat in London's Chancery Lane, where he took on the title of Count Svareff, a Russian nobleman. Using this title, as well as other names, Crowley published at his own expense several books of verse and, anonymously, a book of pornography titled *White Stains* (1898).

Seeking his own end in his quest for magical powers, Crowley quarrelled with Mathers and was expelled from the *Golden Dawn*. A Great Revelation was said to come to him in Cairo where he received a visit from a supposed Holy Guardian Angel named *Aiwass*, who commanded Crowley to take down a message for mankind — *The Book of the Law*.

Aleister Crowley

Crowley's wife, Rose, is reported to have had a demonic revelation in which the number 666 appeared. Shocked by the revelation, Crowley revealed to his wife that 666 was his number. Crowley then took on another name — *the Beast*.

He saw himself as the 'messiah' of a new religion.

Years later, when asked why he assumed the name *the Beast,* Crowley responded, "My mother called me 'the Beast.'" IN 1904, CROWLEY PROCLAIMED THE ADVENT OF A 'NEW ERA' IN WHICH THE EMPHASIS WOULD BE ON MAN'S TRUE INNER SELF, AS OPPOSED TO THE EXTERNAL AUTHORITY OF GODS AND PRIESTS. Do What Thou Wilt became the philosophy of Aleister Crowley. Crowley loathed Christianity to the point where he baptized a toad as Jesus Christ and solemnly crucified the toad.

Though Aleister Crowley identified himself with Satan, after his death a group of Satanists in Latin America conducted a ceremony of execration against his memory. They made an effigy of him in mud and wax, which they befouled and burned, bitterly reproaching the 'wickedest man in the world' with not having been wicked enough . . . ***Satan has again proved that he is the master deceiver.***

Dancing Witches

## The Murray Theory

Margaret Murray, in *The Witch-Cult in Western Europe* (1921), advances the theory that the witches had preserved the old pagan religion of pre-Christian Europe. Says Murray, "The evidence proves that underlying the Christian religion was a cult practiced by many classes of the community, chiefly, however, by the more ignorant or those in the less thickly inhabited parts of the country. It can be traced back to pre-Christian times and appears to be the ancient religion of Western Europe."

*While many writers on witchcraft have accepted the Murray theory, and it has greatly influenced modern witches (and the theory's attraction for the modern mind is itself an interesting fact), the evidence does not really support the view that through hundreds of years of Christianity a pagan cult survived in the assemblies of witches, especially as none of the witches or their investigators ever said that it did.*

*Witches believe that Paganism pre-dates Christianity. While Paganism may pre-date Catholicism, it, however, does not pre-date a creator, God Jehovah. One need only trace the roots of witchcraft back to Babylon.*

Says Cavendish, "There were certainly pagan survivals in witchcraft, as there were in Christianity itself, but this is not the same thing as the continuance of a pagan cult. That the god of the witches was Cernunnos, the Celtic horned god, or Pan, or Dionysus, are enticing but not finally convincing suggestions. What seems more likely than the survival of any particular pagan god is the survival of an idea."[5]

## Gnostics

Before 1900 there was a sect known as the *Gnostics* (the word 'Gnostic' is derived from the Greek and means 'one who has knowledge'), who contributed a very considerable part of the magic inherited by both the Near East and the Western world, who saw the world about them as profoundly evil, as the real hell, and life on earth as a sentence served in a prison. "If the world is evil, then be evil too." said the Gnostics. Some of the Gnostics identified this evil power as the God of the Jews, who is described in the book of Genesis as having created the world and whose behavior in the Old Testament failed to line up with Christian principles. "The good God," they said, "lives far away in some distant heaven, and we on earth are in bondage to the evil Yahweh."

The general basis of the Gnostic belief was that enlightenment cannot be achieved by reason, but is the intuition of the mystery of the self. They held that Jehovah is not God, but a demiurge who created an alien world from evil matter, and that the true God is the unconscious spirit of every man, which sleeps in him until he becomes aware of it. They regarded Christ as a great revealer, but denied the doctrine of original sin and the necessity of atonement.

Until the early '50s, most people assumed that witchcraft was abandoned with the entrance of the industrial revolution, and in recent years there has been an increase in publicity given to the activities of people claiming to be witches. Except for a few, most modern-day witches are people of the work-a-day world who look and dress like you and I. This is what makes them difficult to spot . . . except through the power of the Spirit of God.

## Modern Day Witches

Paulus Grillandus said of the practice of witchcraft: "Those witches who have solemnly devoted themselves to the Devil's service, worship him in a particular manner with ceremonial sacrifices, which they offer to the Devil, imitating in all respects the worship of Almighty God, with vestments, lights, and every other ritual observance, so that they worship and praise him, just as we worship the true God."[6]

## The Black Mass and Human Sacrifice

Human sacrifice is a subject that few, if any, ex-cult members are willing to talk about because of the legal implications. The customs and ceremonies involved in human and animal sacrifices differ somewhat in different areas. Also, in recent years, especially on the West Coast, large numbers of young people are becoming involved in Satanism through rock music, occultic role-playing fantasy games, and, of course, by much individual recruitment. These independent groups are usually heavily involved in drugs, are very open, careless and blatant in what they do, and are not directly involved with *The Brotherhood.* Many of them do not even know the group exists. These are the groups careless enough to get caught in their various crimes of ritual child abuse, human sacrifice, etc.[7]

## The Brotherhood

*The Brotherhood,* a group of people who are directly controlled by and worship Satan, has two major centers in the United States, one in the Los Angeles-San Francisco area, and another in the mid-western United States. "This cult is extremely secretive. No written records of membership are kept. Even the contracts with Satan signed in blood by the members are burned by the high priests and high priestesses."[8]

Satanists infest every level of society from poor to rich, police, business men and women, even government officials. Most attend local Christian churches and are considered 'good citizens' because they are involved in local civic activities. They lead double lives and are experts at it.

They use code names at the meetings and are rigidly disciplined by Satan and his demons. "They practice human sacrifices several times a year and animal sacrifices on a monthly basis. The human sacrifices are most often babies — born out of wedlock to various cult members, cared for by the doctors and nurses within the cult so that the mother is never seen in a hospital — the baby's birth is never registered, neither is it's death. Other sacrifices are kidnapped victims, or a cult member who is being disciplined, or who volunteers."[9]

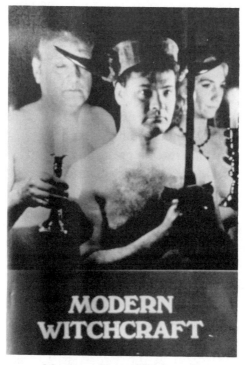

Modern-Day Witchcraft

"Each coven is led by a high priest or priestess. These people get to their position by obtaining favor with Satan by various means and by obtaining greater and greater powers of witchcraft. There is much fighting within the group. There is an elite society of witches within the cult called *The*

*Sisters of Light or the Illuminati.*"[10] There are several occult groups in the U.S. who call themselves The Illuminati, but most are not part of The Brotherhood.

The Sisters of Light came to the United States from Europe in the late 1700's, and have their roots back to the sorcerers of Egypt and Babylon who were powerful enough to reproduce three of the ten plagues of Egypt. They are powerful enough to produce disease and kill people over a distance of thousands of miles by the use of the demonic realm. The witches deceive people into believing that they control the demons but actually the demons are using them.[11] The rapid growth of The Brotherhood is a mark of the end-times we are in and a direct fulfillment of Biblical prophesy.

*Margot Adler,* author of an exhaustive, revised survey of the Neo-Pagan cults, *Drawing Down the Moon,* reporter for *National Public Radio,* grandaughter of Alfred Adler, a Viennese psychiatrist and contemporary of Freud, and HERSELF A WITCH is reported to believe that many covens may 'draw down' the goddess, symbolized by the moon, into a priestess in a trance, who then 'incarnates' the goddess. A priest may similarly 'become' the god. Adler says that she has seen people change under the influence of ritual but that she has also seen rituals which were merely shams.

Judy Harrow, a young woman who earns her living working for the city of New York is said to have been initiated as a witch in 1977. Born in the Bronx to secular humanistic parents, Harrow, at the age of near thirty, found herself increasingly interested in religion. The 'Old Religion', witchcraft, brought the "message I needed to hear," said Harrow. *She adds that it is the hunger for celebration that draws the children of secular humanism to Neo-Pagan religions.*

Some covens, like Harrow's, meet in street clothes, some

Astral Projection

in robes and some 'skyclad' (naked). Witches believe that the build-up of power is achieved more readily when the participants are naked, and when a certain sexual tension is present; they also work naked because they believe that clothes hinder the flowing out of power from their bodies. Dance music and chanting may be used to raise the psychic energy of those in the coven in order to concentrate it on the accomplishment of some commonly agreed upon and benign end; this is called raising the 'cone of power.' The events take place within a circle, often nine feet in diameter, that witches believe defines a sacred space.

It is not known how many witches, *Wiccans* and other *Neo-Pagans* (witches do not like to be called Satanists) there are in the United States, but there are more than enough for Beltane and the seven other seasonal Sabbats to be celebrated around the country. Each March 21, the vernal equinox and one of the Sabbat days, a hundred or more Neo-Pagans gather. In 1987 they met in Berkeley, California at Julia Morgan Theater (once a Presbyterian church), which is located on a tree-lined residential street. At the conference, titled *The Goddess Is Alive,* the participants discussed subjects ranging from different ways of practicing the 'Old Religion' to the nuclear threat and the redefinitions of sexual identity in the light of feminism.

While the 'gathering' is attended by mostly women, there are also a number of young men in attendance; the children are clad in 'flower child' clothing, the older ones looking as if they had just stepped out of a 1950's Greenwich Village bar.

Some Wiccans claim that the traditions of the 'Craft' are centuries old; others boast that they are newly invented. One computer consultant, a witch for 17 years says the origins of her religion do not trouble her. "If something works," she says, "does it matter whether it was invented yesterday?"

One witch says her coven belongs to the *Council of Isis,* which has 2,000 members. The followers of Wicca are so decentralized as an organization that it is not possible to arrive at any accurate count of how many followers of the 'Old Religion' there are. But she believes there are 50,000 to 100,000 active Neo-Pagans or members of Wicca in the United States, compared with about 180,000 Unitarians and about 40,000 Quakers.

It is said that in the early 1970's the 'goddess' movement started as a political statement about feminism, but it did not stay that way. *The surging ecological movement is said to have contributed to the growing goddess religion.* But growth has also brought suspicion and hostility, with members of one group insisting that they have the only true and right way. Intense debates have grown up over such points as what color should be placed where in laying out ritual settings.

Exclusive possession of the truth, says one witch, belongs to monotheistic religions, not the 'Craft', which should hold as its principle, "The only right way is the way that is right for me."

*The radical feminist viewpoint of two witches is, "Imagine that the people of this world finally take that poor son off the cross; let's take him down slowly, pull out the nails and lay him to rest in the Mother Earth . . . never to be seen again."*

This author's answer to the radical feminists statement is, *That 'poor son', the Christ of the Bible, is no longer on the cross! There is no need to lay him to rest . . .* **HE'S ALIVE!!!**

# 9

# SATANIC SYMBOLS AND RITUALS

## Symbols of Darkness

**Amulet**—An ornament or charm supposedly charged with magical power and used to ward off spells, disease, and bad luck, etc.

**Ancient One**—A name sometimes given to an officiating priestess at a Black Mass.

**Arcana**—A secret process or formula; in Tarot, twenty-two pictoral cards comprise the major Arcana and fifty-six (or fifty-two) cards divided into four suits are the minor Arcana.

**Athame**—A dagger, ceremonial knife, used to cast a circle and perform other witchcraft rituals. It is one of the basic tools of witchcraft.

**Baculum**—A witches wand, staff, or broomstick.

**Black Magic**—Magic used for harm, deceit, or destruction.

**Black Mass**—A ritual by which Satanists blaspheme God and ridicule Christianity.

**Cantrip**—A spell cast by a witch.

**Charm**—Chanted or spoken words used to invoke a spell; or an object said to have supernatural power.

**Circle**—The space within which Wiccan rituals are held and where it is believed contact with greater spiritual forces can be achieved.

**Coven**—A group of Satanists or witches, usually not

exceeding thirteen in number, who meet regularly to worship or work spells.

**The Craft**—Witchcraft

**Curse**—A charm or spell designed to cause harm or destruction.

**Demon**—To occultists, any non-human spirit; according to the Bible, an angel who rebelled against God.

**Dianic**—The Dianic cult worshipped a two-faced, horned god known to the Romans as Janus or Dianus, who represented the cycle of the seasons. This was supposed to be the ancient religion continued by covens of witches. Today the Dianic tradition refers to the related worship of the triple goddess (Maiden, mother and crone).

**Divination**—The attempt to gain knowledge of people or events by occult means.

**Esbat**—A coven meeting held at regular intervals, such as once a week or at some phase of the moon.

**Familiar**—A demonic spirit who serves a witch or medium, or an animal that it may inhabit.

**Grimoire**—A book of spells that belongs to an individual or a coven.

**Grove**—A group of covens.

**Lady**—Female leader of a coven.

**Ligature**—A spell which prevents a person from doing something.

**Magic**—The attempt to influence or control people or events by occult means.

**Magister**—A male leader of a coven.

**Magus**—A male witch.

**Materialization**—The physical manifestation of a spirit being.

**Necromancy**—Communication with the supposed spirits

of the dead.

**Occult**—From the Latin word *occultus*, which means 'secret' or 'hidden'; the occult refers to, 1) secret or hidden knowledge available to initiates, 2) the supernatural, and 3) parapsychology and paranormal phenomena.

**Omen**—A prophetic sign.

**Old Religion**—The term for the alleged universal pre-Christian goddess religion.

**Pentagram**—A five-pointed star which consists of a continuous line that crosses itself. Shown with one point up, it is a symbol of the 'Old Religion.' Two points up are supposed to indicate devotion to Satan.

**Sabbat**—A quarterly or semi-quarterly meeting of witches or Satanists. Eight major annual festivals of the 'Old Religion.' These are The Vigil of Samhain (Halloween), the Celtic religious new year; Oimelc (Feb. 1), a festival of winter 'purification' and the approach of spring; Beltane (May 1), the great fertility festival; Lughnasadh (Aug. 1), the festival of first fruits and, in some traditions, the time of the death of the sacred king; the vernal and autumnal equinoxes; and the winter and summer solstices.

**Satan**—Literally 'the adversary', according to Scripture, the chief of the angels that rebelled against God.

**Satanism**—The worship of Satan, either literally or metaphorically, often employing inversions of Christian rituals.

**Seal**—A demon's summoning diagram or signature.

**Sorcery**—Magic, usually of the black variety.

**Voodoo**—An occultic religion that combines magic, spiritism, and the use of fetishes.

**White Magic**—Magic that is supposedly helpful or beneficial.

**Wicca**—In Old English terms, 'a witch.'

**Witch**—One who practices magic.

**Witchcraft**—Today's term used by the followers of the Craft, which means, 'the craft of the wise.'[1]

## The Occult Holidays

There are four holidays that come from religions in which the moon (or a moon goddess) was worshipped as the major diety. These are:

**Halloween**—(Oct. 31)—Halloween is the end and beginning of the witches year. It marks the beginning of the death and destruction associated with winter. At this time the power of the underworld is unleashed, and spirits are supposedly freed to roam about the earth. Halloween is considered the best time to contact spirits.

**Candlemas**—(Feb. 2)—Candlemas was a celebration of lenghtening days and the soon coming of spring.

**Beltane**—Or Walpurgis Night—(April 30)—Beltane roughly coincides with the time for planting crops. The Celts and some others offered human sacrifice at this time.

**Lammas**—(July 31)—Lammas occurs about the time when fruits and vegetables are ripening and the harvest season is beginning.

Four holidays of lesser significance are the solstices and equinoxes. The solstices are the longest and shortest days of the year, and the equinoxes are the days in which day and night are the same length. These are:

**Yule**—(Dec. 22)—The winter solstice, or shortest day of the year.

**Vernal Equinox**—(March 21)—Day and night are the same length with days getting longer.

**St. John's Eve**—Or midsummer (June 22)—The summer solstice, or the longest day of the year.

**Michaelmas**—(Sept. 21)—The autumnal equinox, when day and night are the same length with the days getting shorter.

Names and dates of Satanic holidays vary due to information sources.

## Satanic Symbols

Some of the most obvious Satanic symbols are:

**The Inverted Pentagram**—Usually shown within a circle, is a symbol for Satan; the symbol for the Church of Satan is a goat's head within the Pentagram.

**666**—The 'number of the beast' in the book of Revelation.

**The Upside-Down Cross**—Often used as mockery of the cross of Christ. It is sometimes shown with the 'arms' broken. Another cross sometimes used by Satanists incorporates an upside-down question mark, questioning the deity of Jesus.

– – – –

The following are 'Rituals' from The Satanic Rituals by Anton Szandor LeVey:[2]

### The Self-Glorification

Celebrant:

At once I ride upon a sweeping wind, through opalescent skies to the bright place of my desires. I enter hidden worlds through craters in the steppe's great vastness. There, beneath the cringing throngs, midst whirling fife and thundering timpan, the joys of life are mine to taste. There, amidst Rusalkis' languid song, a life of lust is mine to bear; to loll alone in wanton sloth in crimson halls of dissipation . . . for savage man am I!

At once I am removed and feel the reckoning of my twofold completion. My mind is lofty with the enlightenment of Thy creation! My feet are as the mountain's base, firm and one with the house of joy. My eyes are as a pinnacle that views the scattered multitudes of fools who grope for things celestial; who bow and scrape to wan and sallow gods, the spawn of shallow minded men, forsaking life terrestrial while creeping to their graves. I gaze upon the massive hoards that suffocate, like Peter's fish pulled from the lake of life's sweet waters. To perish in Heaven's foul vapors shall be their doom! The fate of fools is justice!

I am the tempter of life that lurks in every breast and belly; a vibrant, torpid cavern, nectar laden, with sweetest pleasures beckoning.

I am a thrusting rod with head of iron, drawing to me myriad nymphs, tumescent in their craving!

I am rampant carnal joy, an agent borne of ecstasy's mad flailing!

Through jagged ice, my father leers with cavernous eyes, below the sphere of earth that is my mother, moist and fertile whore of barbarous delights!

My body is a temple, wherein all demons dwells. A pantheon of flesh am I!

(Priest receives a bone from acolyte and places it in an upright position between altar's thighs. Priest performs metanea to altar. Congregation follows suit. The brazier is brough forward and placed before the altar.)

### The Great Litany of Desire

Celebrant: (facing brazier)
Great One, hear us now as we invoke Thy blessing: In the pleasures of the flesh and the tranquility of the mind . . .

All:
SUSTAIN US, DARK LORD!

Celebrant:
In bold covetousness, desiring all that might be kept with dignity and grace . . .

All:
SUSTAIN US, DARK LORD!

Celebrant:
In pride in everything we do, display, or are, that shows us not as fools . . .

All:
SUSTAIN US, DARK LORD!

Celebrant:
For riches yet unclaimed by mind or hands . . .

All:
GRANT US, DARK LORD!

Celebrant:
For wisdom to be sown in the fields which bear great harvest . . .

All:
GRANT US, DARK LORD!

Celebrant:
For leisure time in pleasure's own pursuit, in which we may all things eschew that speak of vile necessity . . .

All:
SUSTAIN US, DARK LORD!

Celebrant:
For Thou art a mighty Lord, O Tchort, and unto Thee is all power, honor and dominion. Let our bright visions be transformed into reality and our works be enduring. For we are kindred spirits, demon brothers, children of earthly joy, who with one voice proclaim:

SO BE IT! SLAVA TCHORTU!
(Priest lifts arms high with fingers spread (incendi):)

Celebrant:
Arise, invoke the blasphemous Name The Lord of Sodom, The God of Cain Joy to the Flesh forever!

OGON! TY TCHORTU OGONYOK! RAZGORAISA POSKOREI!
(Priest empties powder into brazier, instantaneous to striking of gong, and shouts:)

SABATAN!
(Congregation gives the sign of shunning (hand lifted, palm forward, to shield eyes) and responds:)

Participants:
SABATAN!

149

(The brazier is removed and the priest moves to altar, hands upraised, and, softly but with great deliberation, repeats the *Exaltation*. The congregation stands in silence. Priest then removes the bone from the altar's lap and steps back from the altar, leaving sufficient room for the congregants to pass before her. All congregants come forward individually, stop before the altar, and bow low. Upon rising, each congregant receives the tip of the bone upon his brow, administered by the priest, who says:)

Celebrant:
Ya Tsyebyeh dayu padarok Tchorta. (The gift of Tchort be with you.)

(After the congregation has reassembled, the priest points the bone towards the Sigil of Baphomet and, turning to the congregation says:)

Celebrant:
Forget ye not what was and is to be! Flesh without sin, world without end!

(The priest closes the ceremony according to the standard procedure.)

The End

## Book of Shadows

(The Book of Shadows is kept a secret. No two are alike. Since it is always copied in longhand from someone else's Book of Shadows no one but a witch would own a Book of Shadows.)

# A CAULDRON RITE FOR THE WINTER SOLSTICE

"Place the cauldron in the South; wreathe it with holly or ivy. Light a fire within making sure there is no light but the candle. *Draw down the moon* (a specific ritual open to initiates only) while the high priestess stands behind the cauldron, symbolizing the rebirth of the sun. The high priest should stand facing her with a candle and the *Book of Shadows*. If necessary an elder may aid him. The others move slowly around and each lights a candle from the high priest, who has lit his from the cauldron. Then the incantation is read. After this the 'five-fold kiss' is given by all males to the high priestess.

"Walk or slow dance with candles. The high priestess evokes the god with her athame, preceded by the 'witches' rune.'

After the rite, all females give the high priest a five-fold salute, and again all females, as the high priest should be thrice consecrated. Cakes and wine, dance and games, if possible afterwards. And if possible, the *Great Rite*.*"[3]

*(the *Great Rite* means 'making ritual love')

## EIGHT PATHS OF REALIZATION

(1) dance and similar practices

(2) wine, incense, drugs, whatever is used to release the spirit but be careful

(3) meditation and concentration — this is the practice of forming a mental image of what is desired

(4) rites, charms, spells, and runes

(5) scourging with the scourge, a symbolic ritual

(6) control of breathing and blood circulation and similar practices

(7) the *Great Rite,* described previously

(8) trance, astral projection, and other psychic practices[4]

### The Athame

"The best known of the witch's tools is the *athame,* or sometimes a sword," says one book on witchcraft. "The athame, or short dagger, is never used for killing or cutting, but merely serves as a ceremonial tool. We are not told how the original athame was consecrated, but a newly initiated witch must have his or her athame properly sanctified. The easiest way to accomplish this is to transfer power from an already consecrated tool belonging to another witch."[5]

The instructions for the 'consecration' of the athame is as follows: *Lay any weapon touching an already consecrated one: sword to sword, athame to athame. Cast the circle and purify as usual, keeping in mind that all tools must be consecrated by a naked man and woman. Place the sword or athame on the altar, saying, "I conjure thee, O sword or athame of steel, that thou serve me for strength and defense, in all magical operations against all my enemies, visible or invisible, in the name of ____ ____ ."*[6] (These names vary from coven to coven. Only the initiate will learn the name of the particular 'god and goddess' when the time comes.)

The 'consecration' continues:

"I conjure thee anew by the holy name ____ ____ that thou securest me for a protection in all adversities. So said me."[7] (At this point, the tool is sprinkled and censed; then the conjuration continues.)

"I conjure thee, O sword or athame of steel, by the Great God and the Gentle Goddess, by the virtue of the sun, of the stars, of the spirit who presides over them that thou mayest receive such virtues that I may obtain the end that I desire in all things wherein I shall use thee by the power of ____ ____ ____ ."[8]

The owner of the tool about to be consecrated salutes the high priestess and the high priest by drawing in the air the appropriate symbol of their office (according to the degree which either one of these officers holds in the coven). The new tool is then placed between the breasts, as the tool is held in place by the two bodies. "The tool should immediately be put into use." Lesser tools are the candles, wand, vessels for water and oil, the scourge, the chalice, and the cord.

Says one believer in witchcraft, "Perhaps the surest sign that witchcraft is a bona fide religion can be seen in the fact that each coven believes it is close to the truth and anyone from a different coven is not quite as enlightened or trustworthy. In time, perhaps, this attitude will change and all pagans will recognize each other as members of one and the same family, the human race."

## Warning Signs

1. Presence of books on the occult, witchcraft, or Satanism, particularly The Satanic Bible and/or Satanic Rituals.

2. Presence of heavy metal albums by groups who promote Satanism or the occult, such as *Motley Crue* or *Ozzie Osborne.*

3. Occult or Satanic symbols appearing on clothing, or books, or in drawings; sometimes a teenager will even draw pictures of rituals.

4. A seeming facination with murder, suicide, or death in general.

5. Secretiveness, particularly on a consistent basis.

6. An arrogant attitude combined with hostility when referring to Christianity, the Bible, church, etc.

*Jesus saith unto him, I am the way, the truth, and the life: no man cometh unto the Father, but by me.* John 14:6

# 10

# PLAYING WITH FIRE

### A Bible Witch

There are characters in the Bible whose lives we can study in order that we may avoid the mistakes they made and the ultimate 'traps' into which they fell. Cain, Esau, Samson and Saul were some of those who got into all kinds of trouble . . . which cost them EVERYTHING! The result of these tragic mistakes ended in the loss of their health, family, and position. Because they did not follow God singleheartedly but allowed the attractions of this world to turn their head they became destitute men.

One man in particular, who was written about in the Old Testament was *Balaam*. This man possessed great talent and potential. Nevertheless, when you read what both Old and New Testaments say about this man, you learn that this is the history of a prophet who became a *soothsayer*, or *witch* (II Peter 2:15). Balaam is said to have been a true prophet who became mentally and spiritually deranged. In the beginning he walked in the Spirit of the Lord and he performed great miracles. But through a series of wrong decisions he found himself caught in the web of Satan. Balaam became a false prophet, a soothsayer or fortune teller, *dabbling* in witchcraft.

Balaam was killed by the children of Israel . . . put to death by the sword (Joshua 13:22). *Balaam had the spirit of divination.* He was a fortune teller. In a matter of months Balaam completely ceased being a prophet of the Lord and

155

became a 'diviner' worthy of death.

This is a warning to all believers *in Jesus Christ, especially those who have entered into a deeper relationship with the Holy Spirit and His power. Unless he or she walks the straight and narrow path all the way,* serious danger lies ahead. There is safety *only* in strict obedience to the Lord and His Word.

In Numbers 22:6, the word of Balaam was so powerful that God confirmed and corroborated it. Everything that Balaam declared came into existance. If he cursed, God cursed; if he blessed, God blessed. Balaam's word carried power: . . . *for I wot that he whom thou blessed is blessed, and he whom thou curseth is cursed.* One of the signs of a true prophet is that God backs his word in every detail (Isaiah 44:26).

We should never be so confident that we cannot fall into sin. It is then that Satan sets a trap in front of us. Numbers 22:20 reads: *And God came unto Balaam at night and said unto him, 'If the men come to call thee, rise up and go with them, but yet the word which I say unto thee, that shalt thou do.'*

This one time when Balaam disregarded the Word of God he did not see the angel of the Lord. Then God helped Balaam out by opening his eyes to see the angel who delivered a message of warning to Balaam. But through a series of events, Balaam became covetous and hungry for power, money and position and disobeyed the Lord. This led to Balaam's downfall. Numbers 22:8 tells the story.

## An Enemy Attack

Not only did people in Bible days disobey the Word of God, so do many today — some even desecrated the house of the Lord.

Even as this book is being written I read the newswpaper

account of the desecration and destruction of a Mennonite church in Lancaster County, Pennsylvania, a farm area which is known for its non-violent, placid people. An article in *Lancaster New Era* by John M. Hoober, III reports:

> "Arsonists tried to burn down an 89-year-old Mennonite church near Strasburg Monday night and 'booby-trapped' the doors and stairwells of the church to prevent firemen from reaching the blaze,"[1] the investigator said.
>
> "Inside the church, firemen found a Satanic slogan smeared on a wall near the main entrance and the altar furnishing arranged in a position to indicate a ritual had taken place before the fire was set, fire officials said."[2]

Reports indicated that firemen found hymnals, paper and debris burning in a pile beside an oil furnace and on top of the furnace. The church's thermostat had been turned up to more than 90 degrees.

Scrawled on a table that the intruders had moved against one door to block firemen from entering the church, was the Satanic symbol, 666. This symbol also was smeared in grease on the wall inside the south entrance. A piece of rope had been stretched across one stairwell and a shovel was leaning against the rope. Another stairwell was blocked by mirrors, furniture and a ladder. Across the inside of one door was stretched a piece of wire, neck high.

Debris had been scattered through the sanctuary. Left on the carpets were hundreds of cone-shaped paper cups. Padding had been removed from some pews and placed on the floor near the altar. Some hymnals, taken from the pews, were placed in a pile in front of the altar. Others were discovered on either side of the altar, arranged in the form of a "V." Toilet paper covered some seats. A chair was propped on top of the altar and underneath the chair, on top of two Bibles, was a Book of Psalms. The bottom Bible was open.

Two pieces of wood, which had been arranged in a cross,

were on the altar in front of the propped up chair. Facing the pews was the wooden cross which had been placed on top of an overturned trash container.

On either side and in front of the altar were three mirrors. Two folding chairs had been propped against either side of the front of the altar. An oak rocker was found at the front of the sanctuary in between and in front of the folding chairs. On the seat of the rockers were three rolls of toilet paper. A baby's playpen was placed in the aisle between the two rows of pews.

Several 10-by-10-inch oak beams that support the main floor had been charred by the fire. The intruders are believed to have sawed off a beam several inches from the floor.[3]

## Roberta

Many unsuspecting youths of today get caught in the web of Satan. Take for example the story of Roberta.

In her book, *Escape From Witchcraft,* Roberta Blankenship, a young lady who had been caught in the clutches of witchcraft says:

"The truth is, it is as easy to obtain a spiritual presence with a Ouija board as it is with a seance. The lights are doused and heavy concentration begins under direction of a medium or leader. Darkness sets the mood and psychologically prepares the mind for concentration."[4]

Concerning 'mediums' Miss Blankenship expresses, "The Bible gives us warning about this very type of thing. *For the time will come when they will not endure sound doctrine; but after their own lusts shall they heap to themselves teachers, having itching ears; and they shall turn away their ears from the truth, and shall be turned unto fables.*"[5] (2 Tim. 4:3-4)

Miss Blankenship continues, "The interest in the occult

is incredible. Recently I was invited to speak to a church youth group where the highest attendance was usually eight or ten people. The night I spoke there were seventy-five present to hear a 'former witch' talk about God."[6]

### Johanna

Having been involved in 'psychic healing' Johanna Michaelsen, author of *The Beautiful Side of Evil,* gives this account of her physic experiences:

"I slowly stretched my body and nestled into my pillows as I began to count down to Alpha. Once in my laboratory, I sat in my chair and surveyed the crystals that shone with the richness of Tiffany stained glass. It was so beautiful there. I turned my chair to face the door. 'Oh, Lord,' I prayed, 'please, reveal the counselors I'm truly meant to have.' The chamber door began lowering—the same radiance shining from behind it—but something was wrong . . . The hair was wild and matted, the forehead was covered with a coarse fur and the eyes were slanted, gleaming and wild—like the eyes I had seen in Playmakers Theater. Fresh blood smeared the muzzle and oozed down long white fangs; the droplets spattered down the front of the tunic. Yet the rest of the figure was the same as before, covered in a long linen robe and gleaming. The figure stood growling, snarling softly as he watched me. A numbing cold paralyzed my body on the bed.

"'Oh, God—let me out—let me out!' my mind screamed, but I wasn't able to come out of level. Minutes (hours?) of suffocating horror. Then, suddenly, through sheer force of will, something snapped and I felt myself hurtled from my laboratory. My body shot upright. My whole system was in shock. I was trembling. I thought visitations like this were over . . . but I had disobeyed instructions. I brought this thing upon myself. 'God, forgive me! Help me!' I turned on

159

the light by my bed. Perhaps my rashness would not be held against me. Surely in the morning everything would be all right."[7]

But everything was not all right, for some days later Johanna would face two figures waiting for her in the lab . . . one was a *fake Jesus,* who had turned into a *werewolf.*

## Johanna's 'Gift'

When Johanna was at college she experimented with the Ouija board. She was given this Ouija board by her Aunt Dot during Thanksgiving — to ease the trauma of her first holiday away from home.

"I was delighted with the board. I heard of it through my studies (she had done her term paper on voodooism) but still had not realized how easily they (Ouija boards) were obtained in the States. As soon as I returned to Wesleyan, I showed the board to Katy* and Jill*, who roomed together down the hall. They were as eager as I to try it, as was my roommate, Ruth*. We spent many hours working the board in a dimly lit room. The sense of a presence would surround us — then the marker would begin spelling out messages. It was all amusing and seemed quite innocent until one evening the presence that arrived was overwhelming in its feeling of evil. The water pipes in the room began to bang loudly and bright lights seemed to flash at the doorway. I looked up and saw the misty white-garbed woman I had seen at the theater. That experience, plus the fact that some ugly predictions which the board had made about one of the girls present had very nearly come true, frightened me so badly that I vowed never to use the board again. There was something dangerous and sinister about it. It was no innocent toy."[8]      (*Not their real names.)

## Rebecca

"When I first met Elaine, I had no idea of who she was, or of her involvement in Satanism. I bought the Bible for her at the Lord's command. I did not realize at the time that I was speaking mostly with the demons within Elaine instead of Elaine herself. She was obnoxious! Or, rather, the demons were. She made me angry, that is why I assigned James (from the Bible) to her first because James has so much to say about taming the tongue.

"Elaine's first stay in the hospital lasted six weeks (Rebecca is a physician). We put her through every test possible and still could not find out what was wrong. I had not learned about demonic illnesses yet and all my prayers seeking guidance in her case seemed to be deliberately unanswered. The other physicians all concluded that nothing was really wrong but I had no peace about that conclusion. Nevertheless she was finally discharged.

"Two days later, on my weekend call, Elaine came to the Emergency Room. She again was my responsibility until my intern came back on Monday. Elaine had the same complaints of pain and illness. It was a difficult situation. I really thought she was ill, but I had no idea what was wrong. Her question to me was a challenging one: 'Dr. Brown, why am I still sick? I even went and asked the elders to anoint me with oil and pray and ask God for healing. Why doesn't He answer? Have I done something wrong?'

"This was a real challenge. Not only did I not know what was going on in her body, but the Lord had chosen to remain strangely silent about her despite my many prayers seeking His guidance. I told Elaine that I did not know why the Lord had chosen not to heal her but that I was sure that the Lord had a purpose for it all. I wrote admitting orders, thinking that I would simply turn her case over to my intern and one of the specialists and would not have to worry about her anymore. However, the Lord and Elaine had different plans."[9]

Two weeks later, both intern and specialist came to Rebecca and told her they would no longer treat Elaine. Again Rebecca was given the responsibility of caring for Elaine, because God had other plans . . . plans for Rebecca to lead this *demonized* woman into spiritual deliverance. The road ahead would be long and hard but the final outcome would make it all worthwhile.*

*A complete account of Rebecca's experience is found in the book, *He Came to Set the Captives Free*, by Rebecca Brown. To order send $9.95 plus $1.50 for shipping and handling ($2.50 if Canada or Overseas) — US Funds only. Make check payable to and mail to: Starburst Publishers, P.O. Box 4123, Lancaster, PA 17604.

# 11

# "TRAPPED"

### 3 Children Reportedly Slain To Make Film
Sacramento (UPI)—A prosecutor said in court Thursday that three children may have been drugged, beaten to death with metal pipes and then cut up as part of a so-called snuff movie produced by five men charged in a child molestation case. Deputy District Attorney, Rick Lewkowitz said that three alleged victims have told investigators that they were present when three other children were bludgeoned in the basement of a house in Sacramento in 1982.

### Satanic Rockers Threaten Our Kids
The blatant Satanism of a foreign rock group, *Mercyful Fate,* a five-man outfit from Denmark, is led by the devilish King Diamond, a confessed occultist.

The group's song titles breathe black magic: Into The Coven, Nuns Have No Fun, Burning The Cross and Welcome Priestess of Hell.

At least two promoters have cancelled Mercyful Fate concerts in revulsion, and a top behavior specialist warns that their music could brain-wash youngsters.

"We didn't know about their Satanic message," says Margaret Barry, assistant manager of The Boathouse in Norfolk, Virginia. But once we discovered what they were, we wouldn't let them go on stage."[1]

### Devil Worship Tied to Bizarre Maine Murder
Sanford, Maine—The bizarre story of a Devil worshipper who killed a 12-year-old girl began last year when Scott Waterhouse walked into a bookstore and bought a copy of the *Satanic Bible.*

It ended last week when a jury convicted Waterhouse, 18, of luring Gycelle Cote into the woods and strangling her "for the heck of it."

Between the time Waterhouse bought the book and his conviction, he experimented with LSD, got heavily involved in Devil worship, became obsessed with a 15-year-old girl and allegedly threatened to kill her, and, finally, murdered Cote.

"The Satanism bit . . . just changed him," Doug Waterhouse, the killer's brother, said when the trial ended.

It was sometime last year that Waterhouse, then a junior at Sanford High School, bought the *Satanic Bible,* by Anton S. LaVey of The Church of Satan in San Francisco.

He studied it and started calling Satanism his 'religion.'[2]

## Cult Investigation: A Road to 'Nowhere'

Attempting to track down information on cults or groups that practice occult worship is difficult at best.

One TCU religion professor with a strong back-ground in various religious practices said, "There are so many dimensions to this sort of manifestation it is impossible to discuss rationally.

"I can tell you about moonies and other major cult organizations, but it is extremely difficult, if not impossible, to try and focus in on something like this."[3]

## Rock Formations Possibly Linked to Cult Activities

Briaroaks—An anonymous phone call concerning 'strange things happening in the woods' brought Gary Puckett, his wife, Julia, and a friend, Carol, down from Arlington to the Briaroaks area last Sunday in northern Johnson County.

What Puckett found he does, indeed, consider strange: Rock formations in the shape of circles . . . with other rock lines apparently in the shape of a cross extending from the bottom of the circle. However, the lines did not intersect to form a completed cross.

Tossed around the rock circle, which had apparently been used as a fire pit but had long since filled with fallen tree leaves, there were bones, which Puckett said looked like large dog bones, or maybe a coyote.[4]

## Johnson County Residents Tell Stories About Cult Happenings

Burleson, Texas (AP)—Howling noises at night, reports of cattle and horse mutilations and strange-shaped rows of stone have fueled stories of cult activity around this Johnson County town.

Residents are divided in their theories of what is taking place. Some doubt that anything out of the ordinary is happening while others are convinced that something is happening.

One woman, Sharon Peterson, became so concerned that she broke the lease on her home here and moved back to Marianna, Arkansas, *The Dallas Morning News* reported Sunday.

Ms. Peterson said her concern began last August when she began hearing rustling noises nearly every night outside her window. One day, she found that one of her screens had been cut.

In October, Ms. Peterson said, she returned home to find a shabbily dressed woman standing in front of her house.

"The woman had cuts on her forehead and one under each eye, perfectly spaced . . . She was just staring at the house," Ms. Peterson said. The woman asked if the other apartment in the duplex was for rent, she said.

Ms. Peterson said the woman asked if she could come into her home. "I wouldn't let her in and that was when she told me, 'I used to live here.'" Ms. Peterson said.

During the nights that followed, Ms. Peterson said she began to hear howling in the nearby woods.

"I was raised in Arkansas. I know what dogs and wolves and coyotes sound like," she said. "This was like nothing you could ever describe."

## Animal, Human Sacrifices Claimed In Devil Cult Case

Sacramento (UPI)—Bizarre details of a child molestation ring that involved 'Devil movies,' witchcraft, mock wedding ceremonies and drinking rat's blood were made public Monday in court documents.

Deputy District Attorney Rick Lewkowitz said investigators were still looking into the possibility that some of the five men arrested also may have produced a so-called snuff movie in which a child was killed while being photographed.[5]

### The Occult—Option or Deviation from Faith

Boardwalk shops of palmists, card readers and crystal gazers have long been familiar sights at seashore resorts. Romantic teens and, more recently, superstitious gamblers looking for their lucky numbers or times to place bets patronize the soothsayers in the storefronts that stand alongside those of merchants offering more practical wares.

A psychic revolution, however, has lent an air of legitimacy to related practices and beliefs considered on the outer fringes of sophisticated ego.

Persons who once would have been dismissed as 'fortune tellers' now appear on talk shows that alternately feature social activists, show business personalities and political figures.[6]

# 12

# INVADING THE ENEMY'S LAND

*And Jesus went about all Galilee, teaching in their synagogues, and preaching the gospel of the kingdom, and healing all manner of sickness and all manner of disease among the people. And his fame went throughout all Syria: and they brought unto him all sick people that were taken with divers diseases and torments, and those which were possessed with devils, and those which were lunatick, and those that had the palsy; and he healed them* (Matthew 5:23,24).

Not only did Jesus preach the 'gospel of the kingdom' but he commissioned His disciples to follow His example and do likewise. We read in John 14: 12-14 that if we believe on the Lord Jesus Christ we will do works as He did . . . even 'greater works.' We can ask anything in Christ's Name and He will do it.

## Destroy The Works Of The Devil

*Jesus partook of the same nature, that by going through death, HE MIGHT BRING TO NOUGHT and MAKE NO EFFECT him who had the power of death, that is the Devil; and also, that HE MIGHT DELIVER and COMPLETELY SET FREE ALL those who through the fear of death were held in BONDAGE throughout the whole course of their lives* (Heb. 2:14). Amplified Version

Christ came to DESTROY the works of the Devil. This

would not last for only the three years of His ministry, but FOREVER. For this reason believers, centuries later, can do the works that He did . . . deliver those who are oppressed.

Sad to say there are those who choose not to believe that we can possess the power of Christ. These people relegate this kind of power and authority only to the time when Christ walked this earth. But this is not what our Lord had in mind. He intended that his followers carry on His earthly mission. He intended that we teach new believers how to use this power and authority. After all, did not the early believers continue on with the work that they were commissioned to do?

Says Mary Garrison in her book, *Binding, Loosing and Knowledge,* "We are to continue Jesus' work, and this work is to SET THE DEVIL'S WORK AT NOUGHT by making it **ineffectual**."[1]

To make *ineffectual,* is to render powerless to produce the desired effect or immediate results . . . To be made fruitless. Never able to get anything done. Can't make it work. Unable to do anything in action. Never able to achieve or accomplish. To work in vain, to no avail, make no impact, impression. To be unable to put into effect a previously formulated goal; never to produce visible, actual results.

Garrison goes on to say, "I should think there would be nothing as infuriating or frustrating to the Devil and his cohorts (evil demons and evil humans), than to fight an opponent who constantly rendered every evil act INEFFECTIVE!"[2]

At almost every turn of the road we come upon a 'work of the Devil.' Should we back away and let someone else 'render him ineffectual?' Or should we use the power and authority of the Word of God to do the job? You know the answer — ATTACK!

## But How Do I Attack?

In warfare, tactics must be used that will adapt to the situation, because the enemy is full of wiles and deceits and hatred. In our fight against our enemy, Satan, we must be aware that he never fights with the slightest regard to any rule of fairness. Ephesians 6 gives us complete instructions, as to the *armor* we must wear when combatting this 'enemy of our souls.' We must not fail to put on this armor, for if we do we will be fair game for the enemy, Satan.

Ephesians 6:14-17: *Stand therefore, having your loins girt about with truth, and having on the breastplate of right-eousness; And your feet shod with the preparation of the gospel of peace; Above all, taking the shield of faith, wherewith ye shall be able to quench all the fiery darts of the wicked. And take the helmet of salvation, and the sword of the Spirit, which is the Word of God.*

As one pastor puts it, "My church and I certainly do not claim to have all the answers, but we have learned that the principles expounded in the Bible still work. Where there is faith (Romans 10:17), appropriated by believers, the miraculous, including power and authority over demons, will still be manifested to the glory and honor and praise of the Lord Jesus Christ. We do not boast. What we know we learned of the Holy Spirit through the Word. God has given the rule, 'Freely ye have received, freely give.' We are 'green' and still growing. I hope we will ever be in this condition, for those who get 'ripe' only hang on the tree and rot. May God grant us never to reach such a peak of 'maturity' that we feel there are no more truths to grasp, no more heights to be scaled, no more wonders to be seen."

## The Authority of the Believer

There are two questions which are frequently asked involving the authority of the believer: "Can Christians command ruling spirits to cast out their underlings?" and "Can Christians command angels to assist in specific aspects of the work of deliverance?" To find the answer one must understand the authority structure of the universe, laws fixed by God.

Jesus Christ is the sole authority for all ministry in heaven and on earth. He "is gone into heaven, and is on the right hand of God; angels and authority and powers being made subject unto Him" (I Peter 3:22).

Ephesians I:1-16 and 2:4-7 tells us the *position* we have in Christ. It is an *all encompassing authority* and one in which His righteousness becomes our righteousness (Romans 4:22-25); *His* life becomes *our* life (John 11:25); *His* authority becomes *our* authority (Ephesians 4:15,16); I Peter 4:10,11; II Corinthians 4:7).

As believers we can **command** and **do** as did Christ:

*Verily, verily, I say unto you, He that believeth on me, the works that I do shall he do also; and greater works than these shall he do; because I go unto my Father* (John 14:12).

Some people believe that just calling out the Name, **Jesus** is all we need to do when we are in a desperate situation . . . Not so! . . . **It is knowing our position in Christ that breaks the power of Satan.** See (Acts 19:13-16).

## The Wrong Idea About Demons

There are those who have a morbid fear of dealing with demons. It is readily known that in war times it is routine to interrogate captured enemy soldiers, especially officers, in order to gain vital information as to the enemy's weapons, tactics, and fortifications. Naturally, one must check the authenticity of this information but to fail to interrogate the enemy would be foolish.

**The Word of God and the gift of discernment** is a valuable tool from the Holy Spirit. The *enemy* cringes when faced with a person or persons who are equipped with the discernment of the Holy Spirit. One question which *demons* try to evade is, *"Will that answer stand in the judgement?"* If the person suspected of having the demon begins to show signs of evasiveness and irritability you can be sure that you need to go deeper into your investigation.

### Demon visits Woman

One must use extreme caution when dealing with demons. However, the same caution and restraint must be used in the exercise of the gift of the Holy Spirit. One can be deceived and led to depend upon visions and revelations apart from the Word of God and unchecked by proper spiritual authority. We must always be on the alert for deviations from basic Biblical principles. It is up to each one of us to be grounded in the Word and not given to 'curiosity seeking' which may lead to error.

*When even was come, they brought unto Him many who were possessed with demons and He cast out the spirits with His word and healed all that were sick* (Matt. 8:16).

It has been said that demons fear exposure above all else. However, Satan will leave no stone unturned to smear and vilify one who attacks his kingdom of darkness with the light of truth and deliverance.

### Know Your Enemy

In the law we are told that the building and worship of graven images is the same as worshipping *demons.*

*"Wait a minute!" you say, I was with you when you spoke of Halloween, but now you speak of demons. Isn't this going a little too far . . . there are no such things as* demons!

But wait a minute . . . when Satan fell away from God he took along a group of followers known as 'demons' or 'evil spirits.' Along with humans who are not "washed in the blood of the Lamb", Jesus Christ, these 'demons' will find their ultimate end in the 'lake of fire' (Revelation 20:10-15).

– – – –

In their book, *Understanding the Occult,* Josh McDowell and Don Stewart give the following description of *demons:*

(1) **Demons are spirits without bodies.**

*For our struggle is not against flesh and blood, but against the rulers, against the powers, against the world forces of this darkness, against the spiritual forces of wickedness in the heavenly places* (Ephesians 6:12, NASB).

(2) **Demons were orignally in fellowship with God.**

*And angels who did not keep their own domain, but abandoned their proper abode, He has kept in eternal bonds under darkness for the judgement of the great day* (Jude 6, NASB).

(3) **Demons are numerous.**

*For He said unto him, "Come out of the man, you unclean spirit!" And He was asking him, "What is your name?" And he said to Him, "My name is Legion; for we are many"* (Mark 5:8,9, NASB).

(4) **Demons are organized.**

*... This man casts out demons only by Beelzebub the ruler of the demons* (Matthew 12:24, NASB).

(5) **Demons have supernatural powers.**

*For they are spirits of demons, performing signs, which go out to the kings of the whole world, to gather them together for the war of the Great Day of God, the Almighty* (Revelation 16:14, NASB).

(6) **Demons are knowledgeable of God.**

*And behold, they cried out, saying, "What do we have to do with you, Son of God? Have you come here to torment us before the time?"* (Matthew 8:29, NASB).

(7) **Demons are allowed to roam the earth and torment unbelievers.**

*Now when the unclean spirit goes out of a man, it passess through waterless places, seeking rest, and does not find it. Then it says, "I will return to my house from which I came"; and when it comes, it finds it unoccupied, swept and put in order. Then it goes, and takes along with it seven other spirits more wicked than itself, and they go in and live there; and the last state of that man becomes worse than the first* (Matthew 12:43-45, NASB).

(8) **Demons sometimes can inflict sickness.**

*And as they were going out, behold a dumb man, demon possessed, was brought to Him. And after the demon was cast out, the dumb man spoke . . .* (Matthew 9:32, 33, NASB).

(9) **Demons can possess or control animals.**

*And He gave them permission. And coming out, the unclean spirits entered the swine; and the herd rushed down the steep bank into the sea, about two thousand of them, and they were drowned in the sea* (Mark 5:13, NASB).

(10) **Demons can possess or control human beings.**

*And also some women who had been healed of evil spirits and sicknesses; Mary who was called Magdalene, from whom seven demons had gone out* (Luke 8:2, NASB).

**(11) Demons sometimes can cause mental disorders.**

*And when He had come out of the boat, immediately a man from the tombs with an unclean spirit met Him and he had his dwelling among the tombs. And no one was able to bind him anymore, even with a chain . . . and constantly night and day among the tombs and in the mountains, he was crying out and gashing himself with stones* (Mark 5:2,3,5, NASB).

**(12) Demons know that Jesus Christ is God.**

*And just then there was in their synagogue a man with an unclean spirit; and he cried out, saying, "What do we have to do with you, Jesus of Nazareth? Have you come to destroy us? I know who you are — the Holy One of God"* (Mark 1:23,24, NASB).

**(13) Demons tremble before God.**

*You believe that God is one. You do well; the demons also believe, and shudder (James 2:19, NASB).*

*(14)* **Demons teach false doctrine.**

*But the Spirit explicitly says that in later times some will fall away from the faith, paying attention to deceitful spirits and doctrines of demons* (I Timothy 4:1, NASB).

**(15) Demons oppose God's people.**

*For our struggle is not against flesh and blood, but against the rulers, against the powers, against the world forces of this darkness, against the spiritual forces of wickedness in the heavenly places* (Ephesians 6:12, NASB).

**(16) Demons attempt to destroy Christ's Kingdom.**

*Be of sober spirit, be on the alert. Your adversary, the devil, prowls about like a roaring lion, seeking someone to devour* (I Peter 5:8, NASB).

**(17) God takes advantage of the actions of demons to accomplish His divine purposes.**

*Then God sent an evil spirit between Abimelech and the men of Shechem; and the men of Shechem dealt treacherously with Abimelech* (Judges 9:23, NASB).

**(18) God is going to judge demons at the last judgement.**

*For if God did not spare angels when they sinned, but cast them into hell and committed them to pits of darkness, reserved for judgement . . .* (2 Peter 2:4, NASB).[3]

174

## We Have The Power!

II Corinthians reveals how we can expose the methods and operation of Satan. They are: *Binding* — II Corinthians 4:3, 4: *Beguiling* — II Corinthians 11:3; *Buffeting* — II Corinthians 12:7. Knowledge and truth are the two forces that have *always* armed God's people for combat. The often quoted verse in John 8:32 says, *And ye shall know the truth, and the truth shall make you free.*

The believer in Christ is able to defeat the foe *because* he '. . . is not ignorant of his devices.' The *church* possesses authority and power to rout the forces of the Devil and to cast out his evil spirits. The enemy of our soul gets in when we refuse to exercise this divinely-given right of the believer. John 10:10 tells us: *The thief cometh not, but for to steal, and to kill, and to destroy: I am come that they might have life, and that they might have it more abundantly.*

Lest you take these words lightly, don't think Satan is going to give up without a fight. He will garner his demons to force you into a retreat. But as Galatians 6:9 tells us, *And let us not be weary in well doing: for in due season we shall reap, if we faint not.*

The gospel of Mark, chapter 16, verses 15 through 18 gives the commission of the ministry of the New Testament church. We read, *Go ye into all the world, and preach the gospel to every creature.* We are to 'believe' and 'be baptized.' Then, we are to 'cast out demons' and 'heal the sick.'

Hebrews 2:14 (Amplified) speaks of the purpose for which the Son of God came into this world: *Jesus partook of the same nature, that by going through death, HE MIGHT BRING TO NOUGHT and MAKE NO EFFECT him who had the power of death, that is, the Devil; and also, that HE MIGHT DELIVER and COMPLETELY SET FREE ALL those who through the fear of death were held in BONDAGE throughout the whole course of their lives.*

Jesus Christ came to *destroy* the works of the Devil. He came to do this not only for the three years of his ministry on earth but FOREVER. However, we must not believe that the Devil is gone from this earth, never to trouble us again. Even though Christ came to deliver ALL who are oppressed there are those who ARE oppressed.

This is where we come into the picture. We, as believers, are to carry out His earthly mission — to both do and teach other believers how to take authority over the works of the Devil.

We are to continue Jesus' work and that work is to make Satan's work *ineffectual.* The word *ineffectual means, not effectual; not producing or not able to produce the desired effect.* Let Satan and his demons know that you will fight —
**INVADE THE ENEMY'S LAND!**

# 13

# BREAKING THE POWERS OF WITCHCRAFT AND DEMONIC CONTROL

Breaking the powers of witchcraft and demonic control requires proper 'war strategy.' A good way to begin this battle is to pray this prayer:

### Declaration of Faith

I come to You, Lord Jesus, as my Deliverer. You know all my problems (name them), all the things that bind, torment, defile, and harass me.

I now loose myself from every dark spirit, from every evil influence, from every Satanic bondage, from every spirit in me which is not a Spirit of God, and I command all such spirits to leave me now in the Name of Jesus Christ.

I confess that my body is a temple for the Holy Spirit, redeemed, cleansed, sanctified, by the blood of Jesus. Therefore Satan has no place in me, no more power over me, because of the blood of Jesus.

Through the blood of Jesus I am redeemed out of the hand of the Devil.

Through the blood of Jesus all my sins are forgiven.

The blood of Jesus Christ, God's Son, cleanses me from all sin.

Through the blood of Jesus I am justified, made righteous, just as if I'd never sinned; I am sanctified, made holy, set apart to God.

My body is a temple for the Holy Spirit, redeemed, cleansed, sanctified, by the blood of Jesus.

Therefore Satan has no part in me, no power over me, because of the blood of the Lord Jesus Christ. I renounce

Satan, loose myself from him, command him to leave me, IN THE NAME OF THE LORD JESUS CHRIST![1]

## General Confession and Prayer

Lord Jesus Christ, I believe You are the Son of God, that You are the Messiah come in the flesh to destroy the works of the Devil. You died on the cross for my sins and rose again from the dead. I now confess all my sins and repent. I now ask You to forgive me and cleanse me in Your blood. I believe that Your blood cleanses me from all sin. Thank You for redeeming me, cleansing me, justifying me and sanctifying me in Your blood.[2]

## Renunication of Pride

Father, I come to You in the Name of Jesus Christ. I know that pride is an abomination to You; that a haughty look, a lying tongue, hands that shed innocent blood, a heart that devises wicked imaginations, feet that are swift in running to mischief, a false witness that speaketh lies, and he that sows discord among the brethern are seven things that the Lord hates and are an abomination unto God (Proverbs 6:16).

Father, I renounce these and turn away from them. I humble myself before You and come to You as a little child.

Father, I renounce unbelief and doubt as sin and ask You to forgive me for entertaining them.[3]

## Forgiveness Prayer

Lord, I confess that I have not loved, but have resented certain people who hurt or disappoint me. I have held unforgiveness against them in my heart. I call upon You, Lord, to help me forgive them. I do now forgive (name them, both living and dead) and ask You to forgive them also, and bless them, Lord. I do now forgive and accept myself, the Name of Jesus Christ.[4]

## Occult Confession Prayer

Lord, I now confess seeking from Satan the help that should have only come from God. I now confess as sin (name them, occult sins) and also those occult sins I cannot remember.

Lord, I now repent and renounce all these sins and ask you

to forgive me. I renounce Satan and all his works; I hate all his demons; I count them as my enemies. In the Name of Jesus Christ I now close the door on all occult practices, and I command all such spirits to leave me in the Name of Jesus Christ.[5]

### Psychic Heredity and Bondage Prayer

In the Name of Jesus Christ, I now renounce, break and loose myself and my children from all psychic powers or bondages or bonds of physical or mental illness, upon me or my family line, as the result of my parents or other ancestors or relatives. I thank You, Lord, for setting me free.[6]

### Loosing of Curses, Spells, etc. Prayer

In the Name of Jesus Christ, I now rebuke, break, loose myself and my children from any and all evil curses, charms, vexes, hexes, spells, jinxes, psychic powers, witchcraft, bewitchments, and sorcery, which have been put upon me or my family line from any persons or from any occult or psychic source, and I renounce all connected and related spirits and command them to leave me, I thank You, Lord, for setting me free.[7]

### Warfare Prayers

Heavenly Father, I bow in worship and praise before You. I cover myself with the blood of the Lord Jesus Christ as my protection. I surrender myself to you, completely and unreservedly, in every area of my life. I take a stand against all the workings of Satan that would hinder me in my prayer life.

I address myself only to the true and living God and refuse any involvement of Satan in my prayer. In the Name of the Lord Jesus Christ, I command you and all your demons to leave my presence.

The blood of the Lord Jesus Christ is between us. I resist all the endeavors of Satan and his wicked spirits to rob me of the will of God. I choose to be transformed by the renewing of my mind. I pull down the strongholds of Satan in the Name of the Lord Jesus Christ.[8]

### Prayer of Binding and Loosing

Father, in The Name of the Lord Jesus Christ, and the authority You have given me (Matthew 16:19, Luke 10:19; Matthew 18:18), I now bind the strongman (Luke 11:20-22) over any evil spirit powers working in and through me and others around me I now bind the following spirits:

### SPIRIT OF DIVINATION
(Ezekiel 21:21)

BIND: A Spirit of Divination — Matt. 18:18

LOOSE: The Holy Spirit and His Gifts — I Cor. 12:9-12

### FAMILIAR SPIRITS
(Leviticus 20:27 — I Sam. 28:7,8)

BIND: A Familiar Spirit — Matt. 18:18

LOOSE: The Holy Spirit and His Gifts — I Cor. 12:9-12

### SPIRIT OF JEALOUSY
(Numbers 5:14-30)

BIND: A Spirit of Jealousy — Matt. 18:18

LOOSE: God's Love — I Cor. 13

### SPIRIT OF LYING
(II Chronicles)

BIND: The Spirit of Lying — Matt. 18:18

LOOSE: The Spirit of Truth — John 14:17

### SPIRIT OF HAUGHTINESS
(Proverbs 16:18,19)

BIND: A Spirit of Haughtiness — Matt. 18:18

LOOSE: A Humble Spirit — Proverbs 16:19

### SPIRIT OF HEAVINESS
(Isaiah 61:3)

BIND: A Spirit of Heaviness — Matt. 18:18

LOOSE: The Comforter — John 15:26

### PERVERSE SPIRIT
(Isaiah 19:14)

BIND: A Perverse Spirit — Matt. 18:18

LOOSE: An Excellent Spirit - Proverbs 17:27

### SPIRIT OF WHOREDOMS
(Hosea 4:12; 5:4)

BIND: A Spirit of Whoredoms — Matt. 18:18
LOOSE: The Spirit of God — Ephesians 3:16

### SPIRIT OF FEAR
(II Tim. 1:7)
BIND: A Spirit of Fear — Matt. 18:18
LOOSE: Love, Power, and a Sound Mind — II Tim. 1:7

### SEDUCING SPIRITS
(I Tim 4:1)
BIND: Seducing Spirits - Matt. 18:18
LOOSE: The Holy Spirit — II Cor. 3:17

### SPIRIT OF INFIRMITY
(Luke 13:11)
BIND: The Spirit of Infirmity — Matt. 18:18
LOOSE: Health — I Cor. 12

### DEAF AND DUMB SPIRIT
(Mark 9:25,26)
BIND: A Deaf and Dumb Spirit — Matt. 18:18
LOOSE: Health — I Cor. 12

### SPIRIT OF BONDAGE
(Romans 8:15)
BIND: A Spirit of Bondage — Matt. 18:18
LOOSE: A Spirit of Adoption — Rom. 8:15

### SPIRIT OF ANTI-CHRIST
(I John 4:3)
BIND: The Spirit of Anti-Christ — Matt. 18:18
LOOSE: The Spirit of Truth — I John 4:6

### SPIRIT OF ERROR
(I John 4:6)
BIND: The Spirit of Error — Matt. 18:18
LOOSE: The Spirit of Truth — I John 4:6

— — — —

There are many more spirits to bind . . . know them, and use the following Scriptures against the forces of Satan:

## SCRIPTURES AGAINST SATAN

| | |
|---|---|
| I Cor. 11:10 | I Peter 5:8,9 |
| Jude 6,9 | Hebrews 2:14,15 |
| Joel 2:32 | Psalm 8:2; 10:15 |
| Luke 10:18,19 | Romans 16:20 |
| Ephesians 1:19,23 | I John 3:8 |
| Psalm 35:10; 142:5-7 | Psalm 139:21-24; 35:1 |
| Colossians 1:12-14; 2:9,10,15 | II Peter 2:4 |
| James 4:7 | Revelation 12:7-11 |
| Isaiah 14:6, 9-15 | Matt. 16:23 |
| John 10:10; 12:31 | II Cor. 2:11 |
| Revelation 20:1-3,10 | Psalm 32:7; 40:13; 34:4,17,19 |
| Psalm 37:40; 97:10 | Psalm 107:2,20; 109:21 |

The Word of God is the weapon we need to break the powers of witchcraft and demonic control. That Word must penetrate deep within our spirit so that when Satan comes to try to unsettle us and cause us defeat we are not overtaken but stand fast on that Word.

# 14

# A CELEBRATION OF LIFE

"LIFE IS TREMEMDOUS!" says Charles 'Trememdous' Jones, author, executive, humorist, and master of salesmanship. "It really is. You can be happy, involved, relevant, productive, healthy and secure in the midst of a high-pressure, commercialized, automated, pill-prone society. It's not easy nor automatic, but it's possible . . ."[1]

These are the words of a 'motivator,' a man who spends much of his life helping others to look at life in a more positive way. Perhaps we need to look at life through the eyes of a Biblical 'scholar.' Then we might get a better perspective of who we are.

Bible scholar, James McRobbie writes, "Man is the crown of God's creation. He is in every respect, 'fearfully and wonderfully made' (Psalm 139:14). He is a tripartite being, consisting of 'spirit and soul and body' (I Thess. 5:23) a threefold being who, in each of these respects, is admonished to be 'presented blameless', and 'sanctified wholly', unto the coming of our Lord Jesus Christ."[2]

Though we were formed out of the dust of the earth we became the image and likeness of God — exalted above the animal creation and capable of understanding God. How sad it is that our innocent children are taught in public and other schools that the evolutionary theory of the origin of man is the scientifically ascertained truth.

Contrary to the evolutionary theory that man is the pro-

183

duct of millions of years of development, and that the story of Adam and Eve in the Garden of Eden is purely allegorical and with no reality, is the fact that our Lord confirmed the historical teaching of man's creation according to Moses. *In the beginning God made them male and female.*

In Genesis, the third chapter, we see Satan embodied in the serpent, in the act of beguiling our first parents. Lucifer had once been referred to as 'the anointed cherub', 'the light bearer', the 'son of the morning.' Isaiah 14:12-15 tells how Lucifer fell from heaven and was 'cut down to the ground.'

Having had your sins forgiven through the blood of Jesus Christ and having been 'set free' from the bondage of Satan you are commanded to serve the Lord and your fellowman with a heart of love — not with the feverish persuance of 'religious' activity, but out of the fullness of His Spirit. Stay full of His love. This will do more than any human effort can accomplish.

To serve with 'overflow' instead of 'overwork' takes away the strain and it becomes a source of joy.

### Joy, Joy, Joy

'America's Superstar Salesman', Zig Ziglar, confesses to being a 'happy Christian.' Says Ziglar, "Under no circumstances would I ever want anyone to think I take my faith lightly or in anything approaching a frivolous way. Actually, I shed far more tears nowadays than I did before I turned my life over to Jesus Christ, but they are usually tears of joy and victory and not of bitterness or defeat."[3]

Ziglar is convinced that joy, laughter, and humor are integral parts of everyday life. He points out that throughout the Scriptures we read references to joy. "In the story of the talents, when the Lord spoke to the two men who multiplied their talents, He concluded the analogy by saying, 'Enter ye into the *joy* of the Lord.' Solomon said, 'A merry heart hath a continual feast.' I believe the old approach to serving our Lord has probably done as much damage as it has done good. If a nonbeliever perceives a Christian as a harsh, stern-faced, never-smiling, joyless individual, the nonbeliever, in most instances, wants no part of Christianity."[4]

## Christianity and Long Life

It has been recorded that according to the insurance companies, the person who goes to church regularly will live 5-7 years longer than a non-church goer. "Statistically speaking," according to Ziglar, "If you dedicate Sunday to the Lord and go to church, He will give you the equivalent of forty extra years of Sundays here on earth."[5]

Proverbs 3:2 says, *For length of days in long life and peace shall they add to thee.* Again in Proverbs 9:11 we read, *For by me thy days shall be multiplied, and the years of thy life shall be increased.* Says Ziglar, "This is Scripturally verified repeatedly. We also have approximately 60 percent less chance of a heart attack and 55 percent less chance of a one-car accident if we attend church regularly."[6]

Serve the Lord with quietness: *For thus saith the Lord God, the Holy One of Israel; In returning and rest shall ye be saved; in quietness and in confidence shall be your strength* . . . Isaiah 30:15. Of all who should have inner peace it should be a Christian.

## The Renewed Mind

Romans 12:1-2 tells us not to be conformed to this world but be transformed by the renewing of your mind, . . . .

"The renewed mind sees life more in terms of parables than of principles," says Larry Christenson in his book, *The Renewed Mind.* "The principles are there, of course, like an invisible foundation, supporting and undergirding. But that which the mind takes hold of, *that which makes the principle operative,* is often a picture, a story, a dramatic image. I have seen the most remarkable transformations take place in people's lives when a vivid image has been used to renew their way of thinking and acting."[7]

The first step in the renewing of one's mind, as given in Christenson's book, is to *build the forms of holiness and let God fill them.* Since we all have what can be termed a 'holiness gap', the Word of God offers some down-to-earth advice about how this gap can be filled.

*Walk by the Spirit, and ye shall not fulfill the lust of the flesh,* reads Galatians 5:16.

Philippians 2:12 says, . . . *work out your own salvation with fear and trembling.* The next verse says, *For it is God which worketh in you, both to will and to do of his good pleasure.* What we cannot do, God must do.

Says Christenson, "The renewed mind faces challenges with the *Authority of Christ.*"[8] Once Christ has delivered you from the power of sin and the Devil you can depend on the Devil to try to regain the ground he has lost. Another challenge is to accept the fact that Jesus' forgiveness goes out unilaterally: Forgiveness goes out to all of us, even without any request being made. Luke 7:48 says, *Go in peace, your sins are forgiven.*

The renewed mind is patient. The renewed mind accepts discipline. The renewed mind prays with confidence.

## Who Is In Control?

If your mind has been *renewed* you won't need to be a 'worrier.' If Jesus, not Satan, is in control of your life you might as well let Jesus be concerned about the things which would tend to *worry* you.

Psalm 27:1 says, *The Lord is my light and my salvation, whom shall I fear? the Lord is the strength of my life; of whom shall I be afraid?*

Fear causes worry and worry causes tension. Since faith is your reaction to God's ability and since God has the ability to solves your problems, He will surely be able to solve your problems — so let Him!

Focus on things that are not seen. I Cornthians 13:12 states *For now we see through a glass, darkly; but then face to face: now I know in part; but then shall I know even as also I am known.*

I quote author Hal Lindsay:

> "Every decision, every act of obedience, every act of faith, every trial endured, will have eternal repercussions. Everything we do in this life is significant and can earn us eternal rewards. Nothing is without meaning.
>
> "In a very real sense, this life is a kind of training for the next. We are being prepared for an external mission in our Heavenly Father's infinite universe. The way we respond to our opportunities to believe the LORD now, qualifies us for our future position and role in His kingdom."[9]

I Corinthians 2:9 states *But as it is written, Eye hath not seen, nor ear heard, neither have entered into the heart of man, the things which God hath prepared for them that love him.*

Because of Christ's sacrifice on Calvary and Satan's defeat, we can be victorious Christians, set free from the bondage of sin.

Now we can . . . **CELEBRATE LIFE!**

# BIBLIOGRAPHY

### CHAPTER THREE
1. Dale-Green, Patricia, "Cult of the Cat," *Man, Myth and Magic,* Marshall Cavendish Corporation, 1983.

2. *Lancaster New Era,* June 4, 1987.

3. McDowell, Josh and Don Stewart, *Understanding the Occult,* Here's Life Publishers, Inc., San Bernardino, CA, 1982.

4. Ibid.

5. Ibid.

### CHAPTER FOUR
1. **Gaynor, Frank, ed.,** *Dictionary of Mysticism,* Citadel Press, New York, n.d.

2. Gruss, Edmond, *The Ouija Board,* Moody Press, Chicago, 1986.

3. Ibid.

4. Ibid.

5. Barrett, William, *On the Threshold of the Unseen,* Dutton, New York, 1918.

6. Ebon, Martin, ed., *The Satan Trap,* Garden City, NY, 1976.

7. *The New York Times,* December 27, 1933.

8. *The New York Times,* October 28, 1979.

9. Ibid.

10. Gruss, 1986.

11. *Pentecostal Evangel,* June 21, 1987.

12. Phillips, Phil, *Turmoil in the Toy Box,* Starburst Publishers, Lancaster, PA, 1986.

13. Ibid.

14. Ibid.

15. Ibid.

16. Ibid.

17. North, Gary, *None Dare Call it Witchcraft.*

18. *D&D Handbook*

19. Ibid.

20. *Deities and Demigods Instruction Manual*

21. *Dungeon Masters Guide*

22. *D&D Players Handbook*

23. *Dungeon Masters Guide*

24. *D&D Players Handbook*

25. *Dungeon Masters Guide*

26. *D&D Players Handbook*

27. *Dungeon Masters Guide*

28. Ibid.

29. *D&D Players Handbook*

30. Cavendish, Richard, editor-in-chief, *Man, Myth and Magic,* Marshall Cavendish Corporation, 1983.

31. Ibid.

32. *People Magazine,* June 15, 1987.

33. *Oxford English Dictionary*

34. Cavendish, 1983.

35. Ibid.

36. Worley, Win, *Demolishing the Hosts of Hell,* HBC, Lansing, IL, 1978.

## CHAPTER SEVEN

1. Wilson, Clifford and John Weldon, *Occult Shock and Psychic Forces,* Master Books, San Diego, 1980.

2. Ibid.

3. Amhed, Rollo, *The Complete Book of Witchcraft,* Paperback Library, New York.

4. Ahmed.

5. Smyth, Frank, *Modern Witchcraft,* Ottenheimer Publishers, Inc., 1970.

6. Ibid.

7. Ibid.

8. Ibid.

9. Ahmed.

10. Ibid.

11. Ibid.

## CHAPTER EIGHT

1. LaVey, Anton Szandor, *Satanic Bible,* 1969.

2. Ibid.

3. Ibid.

4. Ibid.

5. Cavendish, 1983.

6. McDowell, 1982.

7. Brown, Rebecca, *He Came to Set the Captives Free,* Chick Publications, Chino, CA, 1986.

8. Ibid.

9. Ibid.

10. Ibid.

11. Ibid.

### CHAPTER NINE

1. *Insight,* June 8, 1987.

2. LaVey, Anton, *The Satanic Rituals,* University Books, Inc., Secaucus, NJ, 1972.

3. Ibid.

4. Holzer, Hans, *The New Pagans,* Doubleday & Company, Garden City, NY, 1972.

5. Ibid.

6. Ibid.

7. Ibid.

8. Ibid.

### CHAPTER TEN

1. Hoober, John M., *Lancaster New Era.*

2. Ibid.

3. Ibid.

4. Blankenship, Roberta, *Escape From Witchcraft,* Zondervan Books, Grand Rapids, MI, 1972.

5. Ibid.

6. Ibid.

7. Michaelsen, Johanna, *The Beautiful Side of Evil,* Harvest House Publishers, Eugene, OR, 1982.

8. Ibid.

9. Brown, 1986.

### CHAPTER ELEVEN

1. "Satanic Rockers Threaten Our Kids" *Globe,* January 15, 1985.

2. Fleming, Jon, *Rocky Mountain News,* November 18, 1984.

3. Fraser, Rob, *Times-Review Staff,* January 13, 1985.

4. Ibid.

5. Van Nuys, CA, (Los Angeles Co.), *Daily News,* January 15, 1985.

6. Cain, Tim, *Sentinel-Ledger* Staff.

## CHAPTER TWELVE

1. Garrison, Mary, *Binding, Loosing & Knowledge,* Mary Garrison, Villa Rica, GA, 1982.

2. Ibid.

3. McDowell, 1982.

## CHAPTER THIRTEEN

1. Worley, Win, *Annihilating the Hosts of Hell,* Win Worley, 1981.

2. Ibid.

3. Ibid.

4. Ibid.

5. Ibid.

6. Ibid.

7. Ibid.

8. Ibid.

## CHAPTER FOURTEEN

1. Jones, Charles T., *Charles Life Is Tremendous Jones,* Executive Books, Harrisburg, PA, 1968.

2. McRobbie, James, *What the Bible Teaches,* Pillar of Fire, Denver, CO, 1983.

3. Ziglar, Zig, *Confessions of a Happy Christian,* Bantam Books, New York, 1978.

4. Ibid.

5. Ibid.

6. Ibid.

7. Christenson, Larry, *The Renewed Mind,* Bethany Fellowship, Inc., Minneapolis, MN, 1974.

8. Ibid.

9. Lindsay, Hal, *Combat Faith,* Bantam Books, New York, 1986.

Dear Friend,

On the next pages there is information concerning other books and materials published and/or distributed by Starburst Publishers. The first pages give a picture and describe those products which present themes similar to that found in the book *Halloween and Satanism*. Purchasing information is included.

The Publishers

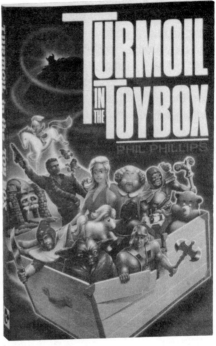

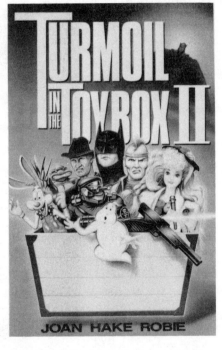

# Books by Starburst Publishers

### Halloween And Satanism     —Phil Phillips and Joan Hake Robie

This book traces the origins of Halloween and gives the true meaning behind this celebration of "fun and games." Jack-O-Lanterns, Cats, Bats, and Ghosts are much more than costumes and window decorations. In this book you will discover that involvement in any form of the occult will bring you more than "good fortune." It will lead you deeper and deeper into the Satanic realm, which ultimately leads to death.

(trade paper) ISBN 091498411X   **$9.95**

### The Truth About Power Rangers     Phil Phillips

An in-depth look at the Mighty Morphin Power Rangers, revealing the violence and philiosophy behind the #1 toy and kids' TV show in America. Power Rangers are leaping off toy store shelves and kicking their way into the minds of millions of children. This book explores the Power Rangers phenomena and the impact they have on children.

(trade paper ISBN 0914984675   **$6.95**

### Dinosaurs, The Bible, Barney & Beyond     Phill Phillips

In-depth look at Evolution, Creation Science, and Dinosaurs in the media and toys. Reader learns why Barney, the oversized purple dinosaur, has become a pal to millions of children, and what kind of role model is Barney.

(trade paper) ISBN 0914984594   **$9.95**

### Teenage Mutant Ninja Turtles Exposed!     —Joan Hake Robie

Looks closely at the national popularity of Teenage Mutant Ninja Turtles. Tells what they teach and how this "turtle" philosophy affects children (and adults) mentally, emotionally, socially, morally, and spiritually. The book gives the answer to what we can do about the problem.

(trade paper) ISBN 0914984314   **$5.95**

### Angels, Angels, Angels     —Phil Phillips

Subtitled—*Embraced by The Light...or...Embraced by The Darkness?* Discovering the truth about Angels, Near-Death Experiences and other Spiritual Awakenings. Also, why the sudden interest in angels in this day and age.

(trade paper) ISBN 0914984659   **$10.95**

# Books by Starburst Publishers—cont'd.

### TemperaMysticism
—Shirley Ann Miller

Subtitled—*Exploding The Temperament Theory.* Former Astrologer reveals how Christians (including some well-respected leaders) are being lured into the occult by practicing the Temperaments (Sanguine, Choleric, Phlegmatic, and Melancholy) and other New Age personality typologies.

(trade paper)  ISBN 0914984306  **$8.95**

### Political Correctness Exposed
—Marvin Sprouse

Subtitled—*A Piranha in Your Bathtub.* Explores the history of Political Correctness, how it originated, who keeps it alive today, and more importantly, how to combat Political Correctness.

(trade paper)  ISBN 0914984624  **$9.95**

### Beyond The River
—Gilbert Morris & Bobby Funderburk

The first novel of *The Far Fields* series, **Beyond the River** makes for intriguing reading with high spiritual warfare impact. Set in the future and in the mode of *Brave New World* and *1984,* **Beyond The River** presents a world that is ruined by modern social and spiritual trends. This anti-utopian novel offers an excellent opportunity to speak to the issues of the New Age and "politically-correct" doctrines that are sweeping the country.

(trade paper)  ISBN 0914984519  **$8.95**

### Nightmare In Dallas
—Beverly Oliver

The hard-hitting account of the mysterious "Babushka Lady," Beverly Oliver, who at the age of seventeen was an eyewitness to the assassination of President John F. Kennedy. This is only the second book to be written by one who saw the event first-hand. Beverly was a personal friend of Jack Ruby and was married to a member of the Mafia. Beverly film of the event (the only other known motion picture) was confiscated by two men who called themselves FBI agents. To this present day, neither she nor any other known person has been permitted to view the film. Why? This book tells the story.

(hardcover)  ISBN 0914984608  **$19.95**

### The Beast Of The East
—Alvin M. Shifflett

Asks the questions: Has the Church become involved in a "late date" comfort mode—expecting to be "raptured" before the Scuds fall? Should we prepare for a long and arduous Desert Storm to Armageddon battle? Are we ignoring John 16:33, *In this world you will have trouble?* (NIV)

(trade paper)  ISBN 0914984411  **$6.95**

### On The Brink
—Daymond R. Duck

This easy-to-understand book on end-time Bible prophecy is organized in Biblical sequence and written with simplicity so that the reader will comprehend this often difficult subject. Anyone interested in history or current world events will welcome **On The Brink** as a handy reference book. Contains topic and scripture reference indexes.

(trade paper) ISBN 0914984586 **$9.95**

### The Rock Report
—Fletcher A. Brothers

An "uncensored" look into today's Rock Music scene—provides the reader with the necessary information and illustrations to make intelligent decisions about rock music and its influence on the mind.

(trade paper) ISBN 0914984136 **$6.95**

### The World's Oldest Health Plan
—Kathleen O'Bannon Baldinger

Subtitled: *Health, Nutrition and Healing from the Bible.* Offers a complete health plan for body, mind and spirit, just as Jesus did. It includes programs for diet, exercise and mental health. Contains foods and recipes believed to lower cholesterol and blood pressure, improve the immune system and other bodily functions, reduce stress, reduce or cure constipation, eliminate insomnia, reduce forgetfulness, confusion and anger, increase circulation and thinking ability, eliminate "yeast" problems, improve digestion, and much more.

(trade paper-opens flat) ISBN 0914984578 **$14.95**

### Dr. Kaplan's Lifestyle of the "Fit and Famous"
—Eric Scott Kaplan

Subtitled: *A Wellness Approach to "Thinning and Winning."* A comprehensive guide to the formulas and principles of: FAT LOSS, EXERCISE, VITAMINS, NATURAL HEALTH, SUCCESS and HAPPINESS. It emphasizes *Maximum Metabolism* through diet modification—fat and carbohydrate modification, coupled with exercise and the removal of sugar, stimulating the body to utilize stored and dietary fat for energy. Dr. Kaplan will teach you a natural approach to food combinations—what you can eat in quantity and what foods (such as sugar, white flour and salt) to modify or eliminate so *you can eat more and weigh less.*

(hardcover) ISBN 091498456X **$21.95**

### Stay Well Without Going Broke
—Gulling, Renner, & Vargas

Subtitled: *Winning the War Over Medical Bills.* Provides a blueprint for how health care consumers can take more responsibility for monitoring their own health and the cost of its care—a crucial cornerstone of the health care reform movement today. Contains inside information from doctors, pharmacists and hospital personnel on how to get cost-effective care without sacrificing quality. Offers legal strategies to protect your rights when illness is terminal.

(hardcover) ISBN 0914984527 **$22.95**

# Books by Starburst Publishers—cont'd.

## *Parenting With Respect and Peacefulness* —Louise A. Dietzel

Subtitled: *The Most Difficult Job in the World.* Parents who love and respect themselves parent with respect and peacefulness. Yet, parenting with respect is the most difficult job in the world. This book informs parents that respect and peace communicate love—creating an atmosphere for children to maximize their development as they feel loved, valued, and safe. Parents can learn authority and control by commonsense, interpersonal, and practical approaches to day-to-day issues and situations in parenting.

(trade paper)   ISBN 0914984667   **$10.95**

## *Dragon Slaying For Parents* —Tom Prinz

Subtitled: *Removing The Excess Baggage So You Can Be The Parent You Want To Be.* Shows how Dragons such as Codependency, Low Self-Esteem and other hidden factors interfere with effective parenting. This book by a marriage, family, and child counselor, is for all parents—to assist them with the difficult task of raising responsible and confident children in the 1990's. It is written especially for parents who believe they have "tried everything!"

(trade paper)   ISBN 0914984357   **$9.95**

## *The New American Family* —Artlip, Artlip, & Saltzman

American men and women are remarrying at an astounding rate, and nearly 60% of the remarriages involve children under the age of eighteen. Unfortunately, over half of these remarriages also end in divorce, with half of the "redivorces" occuring within five years. **The New American Family** tells it like it is. It gives examples and personal experiences that help you to see that the second time around is no picnic. It provides practical, good-sense suggestions and guidelines for making your new American family the one you always dreamed of.

(trade paper)   ISBN 0914984446   **$10.95**

## *A Woman's Guide To Spiritual Power* —Nancy L. Dorner

Subtitled: *Through Scriptural Prayer.* Do your prayers seem to go "against a brick wall?" Does God sometimes seem far away or non-existent? If your answer is "Yes," *You* are not alone. Prayer must be the cornerstone of your relationship to God. "This book is a powerful tool for anyone who is serious about prayer and discipleship."—Florence Littauer

(trade paper)   ISBN 0914984470   **$9.95**

## From Grandma With Love
—Ann Tuites

Subtitled—*Thoughts For Her Children Everywhere.* Offers practical, emotional and spiritual support to anyone who has an aging relative in need of loving care. Gives hope to those who are crying out for help with personal relationships within their family.

(hard cover)  ISBN 0914984616  **$14.95**

## Purrables
—Alma Barkman

Subtitled: *Words of Wisdom From the World of a Cat.* This book was derived from the antics of the family cat, Sir Purrcival van Mouser. The author has taken anecdotal material used in a weekly humor column and combined it with Scriptural truths from the book of *Proverbs.* **Purrables** is an inspirational self-help book, with a unique slant. Sir Purrcival van Mouser draws the reader into consideration of spiritual truths as they apply to everyday living. The humorous behavior of the cat is used to draw a parallel with our own experience or attitude, and the application is summarized by an appropriate proverb. **Purrables** especially appeals to anyone who loves a cat and would therefore enjoy reading truth from a different *purr*spective.

(trade paper)  ISBN 0914984535  **$6.95**

## Winning At Golf
—David A. Smith

Addresses the growing needs of aspiring young golfers yearning for correct instruction, positive guidance, and discipline. It is an attempt not only to increase the reader's knowledge of the swing, but also sets forth to inspire and motivate the reader to a new and rewarding way of life. **Winning at Golf** relays the teaching of Buck White, the author's mentor and a tour winner many times over. It gives instruction to the serious golfer and challenges the average golfer to excel.

(trade paper)  ISBN 0914984462  **$9.95**

## Purchasing Information

Listed books are available from your favorite Bookstore, either from current stock or special order. To assist bookstore in locating your selection, be sure to give title, author, and ISBN #. If unable to purchase from the bookstore you may order direct from STARBURST PUBLISHERS. When ordering enclose full payment plus $2.50* for shipping and handling ($3.00* if Canada or Overseas). Payment in US Funds only. Please allow two to three weeks minimum (longer overseas) for delivery. Make checks payable to and mail to STARBURST PUBLISHERS, P.O. Box 4123, LANCASTER, PA 17604. Credit card orders may also be placed by calling 1-800-441-1456 (credit card orders only), Mon–Fri. 8 AM–5PM Eastern Time. **Prices subject to change without notice.**